THE STRIKE OF '28

D1604793

New Bedford's Struggle Was Not in Vain

THE STRIKE OF '28

TEXT BY

DANIEL GEORGIANNA

WITH

ROBERTA HAZEN AARONSON

IN ASSOCIATION WITH

LABOR EDUCATION CENTER
UNIVERSITY OF MASSACHUSETTS DARTMOUTH

Spinner Publications, Inc.

New Bedford, Massachusetts

To
Dora Bastarache
(1915–1988)

Cataloguing-in-Publication Data
Georgianna, Daniel, 1943–
The Strike of '28, by Daniel Georgianna with Roberta Hazen Aaronson.
New Bedford, Spinner Publications, Inc., 1993.
160 p., illus., 26 cm.
1. Labor History—Massachusetts—Textiles.
2. Textile manufacturing—History—Unions in America.
3. New Bedford—History—Labor
I. Title
Library of Congress Catalogue Number: 93-086138
ISBN: 0932027-156 cloth
ISBN: 0932027-172 paper

Book Design, Electronic Typesetting, Image Editing & Scanning:
Joseph D. Thomas & John K. Robson

Printed in the United States of America by a union-represented company

© 1993 by Spinner Publications, Inc.
All Rights Reserved • First Printing, 1993

ACKNOWLEDGMENTS

We hope *The Strike of '28* successfully portrays the character, courage and good humor of the thousands of people who went on strike for six months in 1928. They have much to tell us. We also would like to pay tribute to the writers and photographers, mostly unknown to us, who recorded the events.

The Strike of '28 is the result of a long and close collaboration between the Dubin Labor Education Center at UMass Dartmouth and Spinner Publications. We received constant encouragement from the past directors of the Center: Charles Davis, Richard Batchelder, Erica Bronstein, Robert Vitello and from the current director, Jose Soler.

The interviews of the strike subjects were conducted by the authors and Dora Bastarache, Linda Beatrice, Ivan Costa, Dale King, Beatrice Pacheco, Richard Pacheco, Penn Reeve, Sandra Lagreze, Gale Schultz, Jack Stauder and Patricia Stone. The knowledge that we gained from those interviewed (listed in the Bibliography) is the guiding spirit of *The Strike of '28* .

The interviews, newspaper accounts, scrapbooks, private papers, and other published and unpublished material were organized and indexed by Larry Boyce. Many institutions and people contributed to this collection: the Standard-Times, James Ragsdale, editor; the New Bedford Free Public Library, Paul Cyr, special collections curator and UMass Dartmouth Library, Helen Koss, archivist. Gale Schultz, Patricia Stone, Phil Silvia, Robin Kelley, William Isherwood, Paul Ramos and Paul Buhle graciously shared their material and knowledge with us. Gail Dussault and Lois Smith transcribed the interviews.

We wrote *The Strike of '28* from the original outline written by Bronwen Zwirner. Erica Bronstein, Barbara Schermack, Joe Thomas and Eve Sterne edited the various drafts, and Eileen Harrington organized the footnotes and bibliography. Cathy Houser, Marsha McCabe, Bill Schrank, Phil Silvia and Marty Blatt gave us their comments on the manuscript, and Clyde Barrow, Janet Freedman, Bella Feldman-Bianco, Ed Clark, Ann Bransfield, Marianne Matheny, David Berger, Dillon Bustin, David Tebaldi and Don Howard guided us at critical junctures.

Every page of *The Strike of '28* testifies to the skill and hard work of Spinner Publications' production staff. The layout and image editing by Joe Thomas and John Robson, with the assistance of Jane Thomas, Ruth Caswell, Milton George, Kimberly Amaral and Sharon Georgianna speaks for itself. Joe Thomas and Bob Henry helped write the captions.

The following organizations graciously helped fund *The Strike of '28*: Henry H. Crapo Charitable Foundation, Massachusetts Foundation for the Humanities, Massachusetts Cultural Council, New Bedford Arts Council, UMass Dartmouth Gerontology Committee, UMass Dartmouth Alumni Association, UMass Dartmouth Faculty Grants Committee, ACTWU Rieve-Pollard Foundation and Dora Bastarache Fund.

We especially want to thank our families for their patience, advice and support over the 15 years of this project. They are: Michael, Sasha and Noah Aaronson and Sharon, Alex, Adam, David and Matthew Georgianna.

Daniel Georgianna
Roberta Hazen Aaronson
University of Massachusetts Dartmouth

CONTENTS

INTRODUCTION

In the decades preceding the 1928 strike, the development of New England's textile industry looked wonderful—an example of how the invisible hand of the market seemed to marshal capital, labor and machinery to produce goods at a profit and to generate wage earning occupations for thousands. Upon this productivity, taxes could be levied, schools constructed and small businesses founded. Through 1920, New Bedford was prominent among the textile industry's success stories. During this period the city's population peaked at over 120,000 and 30,000 textile workers saw their wages triple in just seven years. Small businesses and local banks prospered as workers spent and saved their wages. The conditions leading up to the 1928 strike marked the end of this era of progress.

During the previous four decades organized labor had taken a strong hold among the skilled English and Anglo-American loomfixers and weavers in New England. Unions achieved a moral standing in the community that faded later in the twentieth century. In the 1920s there still existed veterans of the nineteenth-century labor movement who could recall exalted notions of free labor once defended by Abraham Lincoln. Among the elder citizens of New England cities and towns were those, like New Bedford Mayor Charles Ashley, who had been members of the Knights of Labor, the movement which best embodied this idea of working people's respected place in a democratic society.

In our own era when organized labor has been reduced to the status of a special interest group, partly through its own posture, this earlier era is worth remembering. It was a time when unions represented much more than the bread-and-butter concerns of those who were members. A century ago unions espoused a particular version of the work ethic. They praised hard work and thrift and condemned competition and exploitation. The dignity of labor, spelled out on union banners and praised on countless labor holidays, reflected a popular view that human labor was a priceless resource to be nurtured by the community and respected by those who profited from it.

The strength of labor traditions was evident in New Bedford when textile manufacturers announced a wage cut and the workers protested by striking in January of 1898. Community leaders and even Boston newspapers supported the strikers. They compared the manufacturers' high salaries to the workers' low incomes and accused industrialists of mismanaging their firms and then asking the workers to pay for poor management through wage cuts. This kind of community support for the strike, which contributed to the union victory, was common in New Bedford and other New England cities at the turn of the century.

The economic collapse of the early 1920s initiated a decline for New Bedford's textile mills and those in the rest of New England. The problem for New Bedford textiles was not high wages, but overproduction and the high salaries of officials who owed their positions to nepotism. The seeds of de-industrialization were being sown by the industrialists themselves. In 1928 manufacturers attempted a voluntary effort to curtail production by 20 percent, but most mill owners refused to cooperate. Overproduction continued and so the manufacturers imposed a ten percent wage cut instead. Once again they asked the workers to make sacrifices to improve the industry's competitive position.

Unionized textile workers protested vigorously and the great strike was on. For six months more than 20,000 strikers remained disciplined and determined to fight the wage cut. How they survived seems miraculous when today a strike of even a few weeks seems hard to sustain. Part of the answer can be found in the testimony of Beatrice Pacheco, one of the workers whose valuable oral history has been recorded through this project. "Everybody had a sense of commitment," she recalled. "Store owners let people run up tremendous bills. LANDLORDS cut rents until they barely met their tax and water bills. There was support for the worker because the worker was just getting along, treading water, and no one could see how they could make ends meet with a ten percent cut. People felt the strikers were justified in what they were doing."

If the New Bedford events of 1928 raise questions about the responsibilities of capital to a community, they also highlight old debates about the responsibilities of labor leadership to working people.

Ever since Eugene Debs praised the "Christ-like virtue of sympathy" in calling for railroad workers to boycott Pullman cars in sympathy with the striking workers who built those cars, the labor movement has invoked the need for solidarity in times of crisis. But when Debs asked the American Federation of Labor and the other railroad brotherhoods to join the 1894 Pullman strike, they refused because they feared a confrontation with the federal government. In fact, the policies and practices of organized labor have often produced fragmentation, not solidarity. When foreign-born workers and their children came to dominate the work force in the twentieth century, nationality and religion further exacerbated differences based on craft and trade. Therefore, studies such as this account of the New Bedford strike are helpful because they explain how workers overcame vast differences in important moments of solidarity.

The unity achieved by workers in New Bedford was remarkable. The unskilled Portuguese and Polish workers of New Bedford who joined the Anglo-American skilled workers in the 1928 strike had been excluded from the existing unions. Unlike the skilled workers of the Textile Council who had craft traditions and community status to give them a sense of power, the immigrant mill hands had been relatively acquiescent. They had been the loyal work force the manufacturers sought, working long hours in return for regular wages to be carefully spent, saved and sent home to loved ones. But with the wage cut the manufacturers broke faith with these people. The bosses failed to hold up their end of the bargain, and the immigrant workers organized with tremendous creativity and solidarity.

The 1928 strike was noteworthy because of the role Communists played in mobilizing immigrant workers through the militant Textile Mill Committees (TMC). The importance of the Communist leaders in the TMC can be exaggerated and it clearly was at the time by the employers and the police as well as by the skilled workers organized in the Textile Council. In addition, the Communists called attention to themselves by espousing an ultra-left view that striking workers could be made into revolutionaries. Jack Rubenstein later reflected on the Communists' actual influence upon immigrant strikers. He believed these workers who "had not been represented by the craft unions" were loyal to the TMC as their union rather than to the Communists who led it.

Many of the Communists who were active in this ultra-revolutionary period later criticized the Party for sectarianism and for forming separate or "dual" unions. Historians have been vigorously debating the degree to which these leftists followed a party line or adapted their activity to local contexts. But looking back on the 1920s there can be no doubt of the important role played by Communists like Fred Beal and Socialists like Frank Manning. Throughout this period of history and through the formative years of the 1930s, men and women with radical vision performed a critical service to the emerging industrial unions.

Without leaders committed to a broader vision of social change, the labor movement is unlikely to produce activists with the courage and conviction to take on the task of organizing the unorganized. Certainly one lesson to be drawn from the 1920s is that if organized labor does not adapt to changes in the work force, if it rests on the backs of those it has always represented, it will probably face another challenge from those who need protection but are not welcome in the House of Labor.

Likewise, if the labor movement remains dedicated to bread-and-butter concerns and lacks a political vision, it will not learn one of the clear lessons from the 1920s and 1930s, that organized labor needed to become a broad social movement that shook government and changed laws. Unions faced the combined power of the employers and their hired agents as well as the police, the courts, the national guard, the state legislatures and the Congress. The struggle in the 1928 strike, documented in this book, over the right to picket and the right to vote on the settlement underline the importance of democratic rights to the labor movement.

The labor movement began to revive after the passage of the Norris-LaGuardia Act in 1932 which liberated workers from signing anti-union ("yellow dog") contracts and limited the use of court injunctions to break strikes. Five years later when the Supreme Court upheld the Wagner Act and ruled on cases that protected peaceful picketing, the labor movement advanced. Without a comparable legislative and legal breakthrough in the 1990s, a revival of unionism is unlikely.

But even with labor law reform unions would face formidable difficulties. As long as investment decisions remain entirely in the hands of corporate and banking executives, unions and community groups will be severely handicapped. The story of the 1928 strike, as well as many other labor struggles, shows that bargaining over wages, hours, conditions and benefits fails to address the greater issues of industrial viability and social security. Early twentieth- century unions, even the radical ones, never imagined strikes and political campaigns directed at capital investment and marketing decisions, like the inspiring 1982 struggle to save Morse Cutting Tools in New Bedford.

Massachusetts and its industrial workers have now suffered through two decades of disastrous mismanagement and corporate irresponsibility. Unless the government intervenes and forces corporate capital to recognize and respect workers and their organizations, just as is did in the 1930s, change will continue to be for the worse. Unless capital is made accountable to social needs and unless the government is made responsible for protecting, nurturing and enriching labor, we will continue down the same path that led to the decline of New England's textile manufacturing industry and the dislocation of its workers.

In sum, this revealing story of the New Bedford strike reminds us why the study of labor history has been invested with such a sense of mission by historians. More than most students of the past, labor historians have made a commitment to preserve the stories of working people who have often been invisible in our national memory and to bring these stories to a wider public. What is this special mission that inspires the commitment to tell "labor's untold story"?

This book is clearly the product of those commitments. What is this special mission that inspires so many works of labor history?

First, there is a sense of justice about working people's contribution to society and the economy. In the nineteenth century many citizens believed in the labor theory of value: that those who worked productively were entitled to dignity and respect, to the full value of their labor. And what does labor history show? A record of injustice. There is a strong emphasis in New England industrial history on the contributions of technological innovation, entrepreneurial daring and managerial innovation. But we have to wonder in our own time of industrial disaster whether these accomplishments can be celebrated uncritically. As we see the devastation of dislocated workers, their families and communities, we have to wonder why their "investment" has not been appreciated and celebrated.

Secondly, the passion to tell the stories of working men and women has to do with the unfulfilled promise of democracy in America. Labor history shows how unions consistently sought to expand democracy and the Bill of Rights to the community and the work place.

Third, we need to study labor history—more than ever— to understand what went wrong with the American economy and what happened to the American labor movement. A study like *The Strike of '28* helps us think about history and its implications for public policy. Today's public-spirited labor historians believe that the public should care about history, that by studying our past we can help to shape our present and future.

James Green is a Professor and Director of the Labor Studies Program at the College of Public and Community Service, University of Massachusetts at Boston. He is the author of Boston's Workers: A Labor History, The World of the Worker and other works of labor and political history.

"The Stacks of Great Mills have Replaced in the Skyline the Masts of Ships."

– Zephaniah Pease

The old industry and the new. Rotting whaling ship docked in front of the Potomska Mills, circa 1900. [George H. Nye]

CHAPTER 1

WHALING TO TEXTILES

While the whaling business is still pursued with an energy worthy of all praise...the whistle of the steam engine, heard morning, noon and night, tells where the busy hand of labor is at work.

— Mayor George Richmond's Inaugural Speech, January 3, 1870

On Monday, April 9, 1928, the day after Easter, the New Bedford Cotton Manufacturers' Association announced a ten percent wage cut to take effect the following Monday. The city's 30,000 textile workers, angry from years of low wages and speedups, decided to strike rather than accept another wage cut. Shutting down the mills was the easy part; keeping the mill workers on strike would prove more difficult.

The outlook was not very promising for the city's mill workers and their unions. Few unions existed elsewhere in the United States. By the mid-1920s the house of labor had fallen, and the striking mill workers stood alone. When they worked, New Bedford's mill workers were paid about one-half of subsistence wages, and they were divided on the job and in the union halls by nationality, religion and gender.

But through resourceful leadership and their own courage, the city's mill workers kept the mills closed for six months and forced the mill owners to negotiate with them until starvation and the approach of winter drove them to accept a compromise of a smaller pay cut.

Our story begins with the wealth accumulated when New Bedford was the whaling capital of the world. After the discovery of petroleum, whaling became riskier and less profitable. New Bedford's whaling merchants shifted their money from whaling ships to cotton mills, but they continued to tightly control economic and political power in the city. They procured labor from the immigrants flooding into America in the late 1800s, and by the turn of the twentieth century New Bedford became the largest producer of fine cloth in the United States, transforming the town from a small port village to a bustling manufacturing city with large mill complexes and vibrant working-class neighborhoods.

Yankee Boy Whaler, *pulp fiction romanticizing whaling, 1885. "Americans preferred. The chance of a lifetime. Outfits furnished. Only warm climates visited. Doctors on board every vessel. First-class food and plenty of it. Now is the time." Actual working conditions, however, forced owners to recruit overseas. By the 1890s, whaling crews were almost entirely Cape Verdean, West Indian or Azorean, and most captains were of Portuguese descent.*
New Bedford Free Public Library

THE WHALING CITY

Ten years before the Revolutionary War, Nantucket whaling merchant Joseph Rotch moved his business to Dartmouth[1]. The village, later named New Bedford, was less exposed to enemy warships and had a larger harbor and lower marketing costs. Other Nantucket merchants followed after the war, and local merchants, connected to Nantucket by family, custom and the Quaker religion, also took up the trade. These whaling merchants operated a complex network of finance, shipbuilding, ship supply and marketing through their interlocking control of banks and the waterfront. During the decades before the Civil War, New Bedford became the leading whaling port in the world.[2]

Whaling proved profitable for New Bedford merchants. Although the business was risky, profits were high, and many of the ships paid for themselves on their first trips. Furthermore, almost all of the work was done aboard ship during the long voyages. After they killed the whale, seamen processed its carcass into several products, requiring little investment on shore. They rendered the blubber into oil used for lubricants and lighting, dipped out spermaceti oil from the sperm whale's head to make the finest candles, and stripped the baleen whales' jaws for whalebone used in corsets. Once in port, the merchants had only to grade and package the products and transport them out of New Bedford. Because the ten thousand crewmen on New Bedford ships were at sea for long periods, few had families in port.[3] New Bedford remained a small city of whaling merchants and their suppliers. Unemployed men were directed to the wharves whence, like it or not, they shipped out for three to five years.

A seaman on a whaling ship wasn't paid a wage but was paid a share of the catch with food, clothing and other expenses deducted from his pay. The seamen's shares were small, sometimes less than one-two hundredths of the ship's revenue, and much of this found its way into the shipowners'

New Bedford wharves, circa 1890. Throughout the latter part of the nineteenth century, New Bedford maintained its ranking as the fourth largest cargo terminal in the United States, following New York, Philadelphia and New Orleans. Although bales of cotton, coal, lumber and other commodities increased tonnage at this time, whale oil was still New Bedford's largest volume item.
Spinner Collection

pockets, because these merchants doubled as outfitters, selling clothes and supplies to the crew at high prices. At sea, the captain sold supplies to the crew from the slop chest at highly inflated prices. Often, seamen returned with nothing to show for the long voyage and sometimes even owed money to the captain and the owners.[4] Because these poorly paid workers lived at sea, New Bedford, during the decade before the Civil War, was the second richest city in the state and one of the richest in the world in per capita income.[5]

After the Civil War, however, profits in whaling became more risky. Prices for most whale products fell as kerosene replaced whale oil for lighting and petroleum was substituted as a lubricant.[6]

This decline in profits led the boat owners to reduce the seamen's share to just enough to cover food and clothing for the trip. More and more of the crews came from the Cape Verde Islands off West Africa, one of the early stops on the voyage, where drought and disease made the promise of food, board and a free trip to New Bedford worth several years of drudgery on a whaling ship. Because whalebone prices remained high, the merchants also directed their boats to the Arctic where baleen whales were more prevalent.[7] But this had its risks. Arctic whalers hunted in the South Pacific until late summer and then sailed north to the Alaskan coast, where the ice broke from the shore for a few weeks. Here, whalemen and their prey congregated between ice floes and shoreline. In 1871, ice floes returned to land earlier than usual, crushing the entire Arctic fleet, including 32 ships from New Bedford.[8] Again in 1876, the ice took 12 ships from New Bedford's fleet.[9]

Cutting-in a whale, circa 1900. With the whale fastened to the side of the boat, the cutting-in process begins. This involved cutting off the head and cutting into the flesh, rendering the whale into strips and pieces of blubber. In warm waters, the danger of a shark-fest was imminent.
New Bedford Free Public Library

Pumping out whale oil, circa 1910. Because of the poor economic conditions in Cape Verde, sailors signed on for nothing more than the promise of passport to America. "It was a dangerous job, but when the whale boats came to Cape Verde, they never explained anything. They said, 'You come with us, and we're going to make you a man.' Well, what kind of man were they going to make of you during 12 months of sea like that?"
Arthur Packard: Ramos, Spinner II

Joe Ramos being interviewed in his home in 1981. "But I'll tell you, working on the whaling ship—there was nothing to enjoy there. It was a dangerous job. And what do you make? Nothing. How can you work like that?"

Joseph D. Thomas: Ramos, Spinner II

INTERVIEWS WITH FORMER WHALERS

Two years at whaling and you get some things in your brain that you never forget. We hauled in the whale and tried it into oil on board ship. The whale was winched to the side of the boat and rotated around as two men stood on the whale and chopped off the blubber. In rough waters, it took days to turn a whale into oil. The other guys, the fishermen, they got it easy… Even today, if I go to Fairhaven and get a whiff of fish, it makes me feel sick to my stomach.

I like the sea…but whaling, that life was too hard. If whaling, as I knew it, existed today and my son said he wanted to sign on board a boat, I'd lock him up in jail until after the ship left port.

Our four-year voyage was cut short when we shipwrecked in a hurricane… I was in the fo'c'sle at the time. When a bolt of lightning lit up the entrance way, I grabbed onto a rope to pull myself out. Ten other men in the hold with me weren't able to escape. In the last moments, Captain Hegarty grabbed hold of my hand and said, "Tough luck!" I said, "We're all in tough luck." We weren't able to hold on to each other… There was debris everywhere and men trying to swim about, struggling against the waves. Everyone else drowned except for Jules Durant, who made his way to the whaleboat.

Quite a few years ago they made a movie about Moby Dick. A man came around asking if I would play a little part in the movie which required me to jump overboard. He came two or three times and kept giving me fine cigars and offered to pay me $125 per month. I said, "Look, mister, you could pay me a thousand dollars, but I'm not going to jump overboard from any boat."

— Quinton DeGrasse

We didn't make any money whaling because they discounted everything— food, clothing. But nobody complained. You see, when the ships came to the

Whalers line up for hardtack, circa 1900. After a few months at sea, provisions that were stored fresh at the outset were now consumed are turned rotten. "The water wasn't good either sometimes. It had cockroaches and sometimes the oil from the empty barrels was mixed in the water. But you had to drink it, clean or not. You got to live."

Albert C. Church, N. B. Whaling Museum: Ramos, Spinner II

*Whalemen from the **Daisy** towing a wafted whale, circa 1912.* "We also tried to keep away from the tail because if you got too close, he'd treat you like a football. I was in a boat once that was completely smashed by a whale's tail. We were thankful to be alive every time we returned to the main vessel."

Robert Murphy, N. B. Whaling Museum:
Degrasse, Spinner II

old country, they had everything planned. They would sign up a crew, but much of the crew would jump ship to stay in the United States. Of course they wouldn't get paid. The whaling captains would have to come back to the islands and sign up another crew. We didn't care how much they paid, we wanted to get out to come here. Under the Portuguese flag, they would never let people from the islands immigrate over here. That's why so many people from the islands went whaling. It was a form of passport. So three days after I got off the ship, I was picking cranberries.

Whaling was dirty work, a nasty job. There were cockroaches, bed bugs, dirty mattresses and sheets. We'd wait till the rain came, to save the water for washing ourselves and our clothes. There was a lot of water when we first started out, but when we'd catch the whales, we'd pump out the water from the barrels to fill them with oil. When the ship was full, we'd have to save all the rainwater we could. But we always had a lot of rain.

— Joseph Ramos

Quinton Degrasse being interviewed in his home in 1981.

Joseph D. Thomas

Captain and crew shaping up before the voyage, circa 1920 "When the Wanderer came to New Bedford, the captain pulled a trick on us. He pretended to be preparing papers for us to stay in the country, but he was arranging for us to go on another ship. After the trip, we said no to what the captain wanted us to say to immigration. He got mad! He didn't pay us when we first came here. When we refused to go back out—then he paid us."

Arthur Packard: Ramos, Spinner II

"Virtue & Industry are the Springs of Happiness." Reproduction of the original engraved copperplate of Samuel Wetherill of Philadelphia, the first manufacturer of velverets, jeans, fustians and other cloths in America."

Walton

Carding, drawing, and roving in Samuel Slater's early mills. These were three processes used to prepare the cotton fibers for spinning.

Walton

KING COTTON

While the New Bedford merchants concentrated on whaling, cotton textiles dominated most other New England cities. Almost immediately after the Revolutionary War, Rhode Island merchants, using money gained mostly from the slave trade, financed small cotton textile mills. They typically employed a few families with everyone older than seven or eight working in the mill. Using water-driven spinning frames, these early mill workers spun cotton yarn, which was sold to hand-loom weavers. Wages were very low and often paid in yarn or goods from the company store.[10]

Early in the 1800s, their overseas trade threatened by the dispute with England which led to the War of 1812, some Boston shipping merchants turned away from the sea and toward the swiftly flowing rivers of the interior, seeking power to drive textile machinery. They developed a system of common stock ownership to raise large sums of money for industrial ventures and built mills much larger than those in Rhode Island.[11]

Francis Cabot Lowell, a descendant of a rich shipping family, travelled to England in order to study the construction of the water-driven loom. When he returned, Lowell gave his rough sketch of the English design to Paul Moody, a mechanic, who built an operating model of the loom.[12] In 1814, Lowell and his partners built a mill around the loom in Waltham, Massachusetts.[13] When the Charles River couldn't supply enough water power, they bought some farm land beside a steep drop in the wide Merrimac River and built the first large factory town in the United States.[14] Although Lowell died before the project began in 1822, the town he had planned was named in his honor.

Conditions and wages in these large mills offered relief from the drudgery of farm work in a declining agricultural economy where New England's small farms no longer could compete with the larger farms in the more fertile Midwest. Because many of the young men went West, an option not open to most single women, New England's population was made up mostly of women. Life in the city was more exciting than solitary life on the farm, work was less difficult, and mill wages were attractive by contemporary standards. Lowell and the other merchants saw these farm women as highly skilled and submissive mill girls, who already had spent years spinning and weaving cloth at home and were accustomed to male authority. The major problem was to convince them and their parents that the mills were suitable places for young women.

The solution was a supervised life for the mill girls. Boarding houses, owned by the mills and managed by respectable wives and widows, regulated home life. Church attendance was mandatory, and the mill girls provided their own entertainment, often literary or artistic. In 1842, they engaged Charles Dickens to read to them during his American tour. Dickens was amazed at life and working conditions in Lowell. Contrary to the horrible conditions in English mills that often provided the dark backdrops for his novels, he found that American mills were agreeable places to work, and mill houses were pleasant places to live.[15] Michel Chevalier, a French visitor to the United States, agreed: "Lowell is not amusing, but Lowell is clean, decent, peaceful and wise."[16]

The Lowell mills paid cash wages rather than goods from the company store, and they paid more than any alternate employment. In Lowell, women earned about $3 per week with $1.25 deducted for room and board. Wages in the small spinning mills, when paid in cash, were lower, about $2 per week, with $1 going for room and board.[17] Housework paid about 75

The only known likeness of Francis Lowell, 1775-1817. With Paul Moody, Lowell invented much of the machinery used in making cloth from yarn. He also designed the organization of the mills.
Walton

Lowell in the 1840s. Francis Lowell and his partners commissioned Kirk Boott to buy farmland along the Merrimac River. Land he bought for $100 per acre soon was worth thousands. Lowell's plans for the city were carried out by Boott, a former military officer who had served under Wellington against Napoleon.
Merrimac Valley Textile Museum: Walton

Cover of the Lowell Offering, 1845. Published between 1840 and 1845, the magazine contained essays, poems and fiction written by the women operatives in Lowell. Charles Dickens remarked, "It will compare advantageously with a great many English annuals."

Merrimac Valley Textile Museum: C.Ware

cents per week, and seamstresses were paid about $1 per week.[18] Local school teachers, when they worked, received roughly the same weekly pay as textile workers but were employed only about 20 weeks a year.

Although the wages were only about $50 per week at today's prices, for a woman who never before had any money of her own, these wages meant independence. Also, because room and board took less than one-half of their wages, many women sent money home to pay off farm debts and improve living conditions on farms which produced little cash. Their wages also paid for their brothers' or sons' education. President James Walker of Harvard University estimated that about one-quarter of his students received money from sisters or mothers in the mills.[19]

Harriet Hanson Robinson, who began work in the Lowell mills at the age of ten in 1835, remembered mill work as women's liberation rather than exploitation. In 1889, looking back across 60 years to her experience in the mills, she described the reawakening of women, considered encumbrances at home:

> I can see them now, even after sixty years, just as they looked,—depressed, modest, mincing, hardly daring to look one in the face, so shy and sylvan had been their lives. But after the first payday came, and they felt the jingle of silver in their pockets and had begun to feel its mercurial influence, their bowed heads were lifted, their necks seemed braced with steel, they looked you in the face, sang blithely among their looms or frames and walked with elastic step to and from their work... It seemed a great hope impelled them — the harbinger of a new era that was about to dawn for them and for all women-kind.[20]

The mill girls fought to keep their independence. In 1834, the mill owners claimed that a slump in the cloth market and rising prices for raw cotton forced them to cut wages and increase the work pace.[21] The mill girls

"New England Factory Life — Bell Time," by Winslow Homer, 1868. Like most intellectuals of his time, Homer believed that the mills were destroying New England country life, which previously had obeyed only the cycle of nature but now was ruled by factory bells. "We know of no more sadder sight on earth than our factory villages presents; when the bell at the break of day, or breakfast or dinner, calls out its hundreds or thousands of operatives."

Merrimac Valley Textile Museum: Brownson, Robinson

proved themselves more independent than the mill owners wanted and walked off the job. Largely unorganized, the strike was broken after a few days, but two years later the Lowell workers struck again over an increase in room and board at the mill boarding houses and a wage cut amounting to about 30 percent.[22] This time the strikers formed an organization called the Factory Girls Association that claimed 2,500 members, but once again most bowed to the power of the mill owners and returned to work after a few days. The Factory Girls Association soon disappeared.[23]

Working conditions in the mills and life in the boarding houses deteriorated, but the expansion of the industry continued and even accelerated. Advertising and word of mouth no longer brought farm women into the mills, especially because the message that defecting mill workers brought back to their villages was of falling pay and harsher conditions. The mill owners began using labor contractors to bring workers from the far reaches of New England at $1 per head.[24] When this wasn't enough to satisfy the need for labor, the mill owners began hiring immigrants. In the early days, the daughters and wives of the Irish workmen who had built the city hadn't been considered worthy to work alongside American women in the mills; but labor shortages led the mill owners to hire Irish women, and the labor contractors spread their nets into French-speaking Canada.[25]

U.S. cotton textile production more than doubled between 1840 and 1860.[26] By the start of the Civil War, the cotton textile industry dominated the cities and towns of New England with 600 cotton textile mills throughout the region.[27] But the Civil War marked the beginning of the end for New England's domination in cotton textiles. The destruction of the plantation system provided the incentive for the development of large-scale manufacturing in the South, and following the usual sequence of the industrial revolution, cotton textiles led the way.

The South held several advantages over the North in attracting investment to textile production. Mill wages were lower in the South, where falling prices for cotton caused by the fierce competition between black and white sharecroppers drove whole families into the mills. Dire poverty forced them to accept almost any wages and working conditions. The brutal policy of segregation was another advantage. Mill owners could threaten to replace white workers, predominant in southern mills, with readily available, destitute black workers. Furthermore, social legislation in the North pushed capital toward the South, where virtually no laws restricted long work weeks, child labor and night work for women. Finally, southern mill owners held the advantage of technological improvements. They installed the newest, most advanced machines and technology, whereas northern mill owners resisted installing new equipment, because they already had paid for their old machinery.[28]

The southern mills specialized in the easily produced, coarsely woven cloth, leaving an opening for New Bedford to produce fine cloth.

Woodcut by Winslow Homer of a weaver winding a bobbin. This illustration was made for the "Song of the Sower" by William Cullen Bryant.
Merrimac Valley Textile Museum: Dunwell

Fling wide the grain for those who throw
The clanking shuttle to and fro,
In the long row of humming rooms,
And into the ponderous masses wind
The web that, from a thousand looms,
Come forth to clothe mankind.

Joseph Grinnell, Quaker whaling merchant and founder of Wamsutta Mills, circa 1885. "By intelligent specialization they escaped the commercial extinction that overtook the smaller Massachusetts seaports, and instead of awaiting the inevitable decline of whaling, they chose the very height of its prosperity to give a new hostage to fortune — the Wamsutta cotton mill."
New Bedford Free Public Library: Morison

THE RISE OF A COTTON MILL CITY

In the decades after the Civil War, the New Bedford whaling merchants, weary of the risk and low profits from whaling, followed the siren song to textiles. They set sail together, just as they had learned to reduce competition in the whaling trade by working together. In order to avoid competition with the rest of New England and the South, they decided to specialize in fine cotton cloth, following the pioneering cotton firm in New Bedford, the Wamsutta Mills.[29]

In 1846, the year that New Bedford was incorporated as a city, Abraham Howland chartered the Wamsutta as a joint stock company for cotton production. Although he managed to sell some shares to members of his powerful family, Howland was able to raise only $60,000, less than one percent of the total investment in the New Bedford fleet, so he passed the company's charter to his cousin Joseph Grinnell, member of Congress and one of the most powerful people in the city.[30] Thomas Bennett, a young relative through the Howland line who had studied textile production in the South, persuaded Grinnell to invest in textiles. Bennett suggested the South as the location, but Grinnell favored New Bedford because he anticipated the growing division between North and South and wanted to keep his capital at home. The Civil War justified Grinnell's fears when the Confederacy seized northern-owned assets in the South.[31]

Although Grinnell and Bennett struggled to interest the wealthy whaling merchants, they were able to raise only $160,000, which was barely enough to construct the mill. The merchants hesitated to buy stock because whaling still paid handsome returns, and the New Bedford Steam Mill Company, the city's first textile mill started by Samuel Rodman three

"Wamsutta Mills," oil painting by William Allen Wall, circa 1850. The wealthy port of New Bedford was home to many renowned nineteenth-century artists such as Albert Bierstadt, Albert Van Beest and Albert Ryder. Wall depicts a cheery factory in a pastoral Eden, conveying a mood of optimism and hope. "The Moral history of the establishment of the Wamsutta Steam Cotton Factory is the creation of an industry of which the families of sailors and mechanics could avail themselves, independent of the precarious yield from following the seas."
New Bedford Whaling Museum: Willis

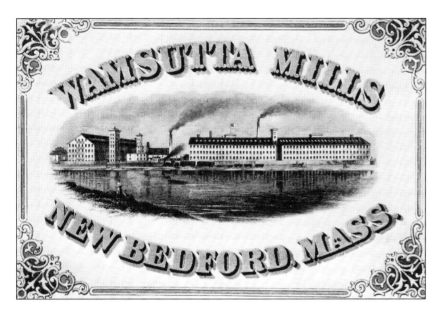

Wamsutta Mills cloth label. "A shrewd citizen seldom died whose estate did not contain at least a share or two of Wamsutta stock — just as no competent housewife would be without Wamsutta sheeting, which in those days she purchased in 40-inch widths and stitched together."

Hough

years earlier, was losing money. Amidst the skepticism of most of their peers, Grinnell and Bennett completed the first mill building in 1848, the same year that Abraham Howland, who never had bought Wamsutta stock, became New Bedford's first mayor.[32]

Rodman's company failed and its assets were sold at auction in 1851, but the Wamsutta confounded its critics and succeeded. In January 1850, the company paid its first dividend, five percent of the stock value.[33] Capital in the Wamsutta grew steadily, attracted by the high returns during the Civil War. In the mill's first 25 years, investment grew to $2,000,000 and the company was producing some 20,000,000 yards of cloth per year and paying a steady six percent dividend.[34]

Even though the Wamsutta prospered, most of the city's capital remained in whaling until after the loss of the Arctic fleet in 1871, when more merchant capital flowed into textiles to build the Potomska Mills. After hesitating for another ten years and enduring another Arctic catastrophe, the majority of whaling merchants abandoned the now high-risk and low-profit whaling industry and quickly moved to the safe six to eight percent dividend from textiles. From 1881 to the beginning of World War I, 32 cotton manufacturing companies were incorporated, worth $100,000,000 and employing 30,000 people.[35] During the first third of the twentieth century, until the industry's collapse during the Great Depression of the 1930s, about 90 percent of the city's manufacturing employees worked in cotton textiles.[36] New Bedford continued as a one-industry town, simply switching from whaling to textiles.

The merchant families that had built their wealth through whaling and now owned the textile mills continued to dominate New Bedford's finance and commerce. They stayed with the policy of joint ownership that they had used in whaling to mediate against competition and to provide insurance against loss. But the city's structure changed dramati-

Percale label from Wamsutta Mills. "In 1876, a young Vanderbilt woman entered the store of Arnold, Constable & Co. of New York and put down on the counter a white closely-woven cloth that she found in Paris. It was called 'percall.' The famous cloth-merchants had never seen such a fine sheeting but advised that if the sample were sent to New Bedford perhaps Wamsutta Mills could duplicate it. After experimenting and manufacturing 50-yard bolts on trial, Wamsutta rewarded the Vanderbilts with percale sheeting."

Hough

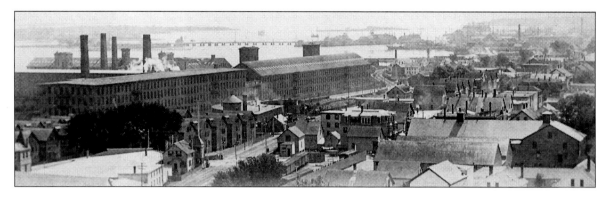

View of the Wamsutta Mills around 1890, looking south. *Where 30 years earlier the mills were surrounded by pastoral lands, by the 1880s they were flanked by worker housing and rail yards. This neighborhood, called Holy Acre, was home to Irish, Italian, French and Portuguese workers.*
Bill Boucher

cally because the city's workers lived in town rather than on the whaling ships and were paid a weekly wage rather than a share of the catch at the end of the three- to five-year voyage. Stores sprung up, selling food, clothing and other essentials to the city's rapidly growing population. New Bedford changed from a port city of whaling merchant families and itinerant seamen to a bustling industrial city. Between 1880 and 1920, New Bedford's population tripled to over 120,000.

In those days the mills were owned by families. The mill owners lived in the best part of the city and we could recognize who they were. They ran the city. They elected the mayors. In fact one of the mill owners of Hathaway Mills became a mayor later on.

— Joe Figueiredo

Most of the newcomers were immigrants. In 1865, only 14 percent of the city's population was foreign-born, but by 1900, the percentage had grown to over 40 percent.[37] Three-quarters of New Bedford's mill workers were immigrants.[38] Although they carried with them a complex array of

Manuel Sousa and family, 1911. "On right end is brother-in-law; next is his father who works on the river; next is Manuel (appears to be 12 years old). He has been a cleaner in the Holmes Mill for two years. John, Manuel's brother (next to him) works in the City Mill." *Lewis Hine visited New Bedford and Fall River in 1911, 1912 and 1916 while working for the National Child Labor Committee.*

Lewis W. Hine

cultures and religions, immigrant groups in the mills usually were classified into simple nationalities: English, Irish and German, who arrived first, followed by French-Canadian, Polish, Syrian and Portuguese.[39] Typically, Polish meant any European from east of Germany, and Syrian meant someone from the Middle East. However, by the end of the century most of the immigrants coming to New Bedford were from Portugal or its islands—Madeira, the Azores and Cape Verde—and almost always went directly into the mills.

Very few African Americans worked in the early cotton mills. In 1900, only 25 of the city's 11,006 mill workers were African Americans, although this probably didn't include Cape Verdeans.[40] Earlier, in 1860, New Bedford had a larger percentage of African Americans than any other New England city. New Bedford, because of its port and its Quaker heritage, was a station on the underground railroad leading slaves to freedom, and African Americans were a common sight on city streets and in city schools.[41] In 1837 Frederick Douglass escaped from Maryland to New Bedford, found friends there, and began his career as an abolitionist, women's rights supporter and labor advocate. But Douglass faced discrimination on the docks, his skin color often costing him employment, and he left the city in 1841. The discrimination he left behind continued in the cotton mills, where African Americans could find employment only if no European could be found for the job.

The barkentine Savoia *in New Bedford on October 5, 1914, after a 45-day journey with 155 passengers and 28 crew members. Over 18,000 Cape Verdeans entered this port between 1900 and 1920, when hundreds of trans-Atlantic voyages were made. Because of discrimination, few Cape Verdeans worked in textile mills and worked instead in construction, maritime trades or on cranberry bogs. Today, about 12,000 Cape Verdeans live in New Bedford — the largest number in any city or town outside the Cape Verde Islands.*
Standard-Times: Boss, Spinner IV

Whitman Mills and typical three-decker worker housing, circa 1900. Like most New Bedford mills, the Whitman Mill was self-contained, making its product from raw cotton to finished goods under one roof. This mill was the first in New Bedford established by outside owners.

Joseph Tirrell

South End of New Bedford, 1985. The clock tower of the Berkshire Hathaway Mill stands above the wooden tenements that housed many of its workers. Most of these houses, in an area covering about 30 city blocks, were built between 1901 and 1911. During the textile boom, mill owners developed much of the sea shore in the South End, an area where wealthy residents once raced chariots.

Joseph D. Thomas

Although mills generally occupied the centers of early industrial cities, most of New Bedford's mills were built in the north and south sections of the city along the river and the railroad lines. Finance and commerce left over from whaling continued to dominate the center, and most of the city's elite continued living in spacious neighborhoods near the financial district, free from the noise, grime and congestion of industrial life.[42] Densely populated working-class neighborhoods grew around the mills in the city's North and South ends.

Howland Village, circa 1910. Built by William Howland as a model village with ideal living conditions, the village consisted of 50 single-family Dutch colonial homes. It was laid out in a circular park-like plan with each unit having its own yard, garden and bathroom. Financial difficulties at the Howland Mills resulted in Howland's apparent suicide, and the housing was sold to private individuals.

Whitney: McMillan

In order to attract the skilled workers needed to manufacture fine cloth, owners of the early mills built housing near the mills.[43] Usually they supplied only very basic housing, but in 1889 William Howland, owner of three yarn mills, built commodious single-family houses with gardens and open spaces and charged rents affordable even to unskilled workers.[44] However, Howland eventually went bankrupt, and his project was the last large-scale mill housing built by New Bedford's mill owners.[45] Housing took up precious capital and reduced the flexibility of the mill owners, because they couldn't easily lay off workers living in company housing. Eviction wasn't a difficult legal procedure, but it posed political and social problems for the mill owners. A few mill owners and most of the city's population retained the social consciousness of an earlier time, when New Bedford was a closely knit merchant town, strongly influenced by Quaker tolerance. During the industry's early years, mill owners didn't evict workers during strikes and often didn't try to collect rent until strikes ended.[46]

Mill housing along North Front Street, near the Wamsutta Mills, circa 1905. Of brick construction, these houses consisted of four tenements with shared toilets in the cellars.

Whitney: 1911 New Bedford Atlas

During the period of New Bedford's largest growth, almost all new housing was supplied by small-scale landlords, often mill workers themselves, who built two- and three-decker tenements. Most apartments were crowded, and many people took in boarders.[47] Cots in the kitchen were a common sight. The increase in housing drove down rents and reduced the profits to landlords. The quality of mill-owned housing deteriorated along with the decline in profits, and by the end of World War I the mill owners had sold their few remaining tenements.[48]

New Bedford's mill workers usually preferred but sometimes were forced to live among their own kind, and they settled into a mosaic of ethnic neighborhoods centered around the mills.

> *We had ghettos. The South End of the city was where most of the English workers lived. The Portuguese also lived in the South End, but also in the North End. The Cape Verdeans were mostly in the South End; there was a ghetto of Cape Verdeans within that ghetto. Then you had the Poles. Most of the Poles were spread out, but the biggest Polish group was in the North End of the city.*
> — Joe Figueiredo

In order to afford the barest necessities, both parents and their children had to work in the mills. Men held the better jobs at higher pay, but neither men nor women could support a family on a single wage.[49] Children, sometimes as young as ten years old, doffed the full bobbins off

Kitchen/living room of family of Alfred Benoit, 191 North Front Street, 1912. The U.S. Bureau of Labor Statistics published an index for the "minimum budget necessary to maintain a worker's family of 5 in health and decency." The average wage in New Bedford's textile industry covered about one-half of this budget.

Lewis W. Hine

the spinning frames, cleaned around the machinery, and did other repetitive, simple tasks. Children learning a skill such as weaving were taught by their parents or other relatives on the job without pay.[50]

> *When I went in at 14 (in 1916), I learned with my mother, who was working in the old Pierce Mill, and I stayed with her helping and learning to weave. I didn't get a job of my own until I was 16. For two years I got no pay. She learned to weave in England, and then she came to America. My father was also a weaver and a second hand.*
>
> — Alice Green

Many children, especially those of Portuguese, Polish and French-Canadian descent, didn't survive to work in the mills. Infant mortality rates were very high in mill cities, and New Bedford had one of the highest rates of infant deaths. One out of every five children born into low-wage mill families in New Bedford died before their first birthday, whereas in the highest income bracket only one out of 17 died in infancy.[51] Children's deaths from gastric, respiratory and intestinal diseases, usually associated with poverty and preventable through better nutrition, were among the highest in the country.[52]

Pay was low, hours were long and work was hard. In order to better their lot, New Bedford mill workers almost from the beginning organized themselves into unions.

Young sweepers in the spinning room of the Bennett Mill, 1911. "They called us kids the 'forty-hour kids.' We could only work short until we got to be sixteen and then we could go the full schedule, which was fifty-four hours."

Lewis W. Hine: Isherwood

Woe to the operative
when agitation ceases.

– Samuel Gompers

"Portuguese Spinner." American Linen Co., Fall River, June 1916. [Lewis W. Hine]

CHAPTER 2

TEXTILE MILL WORKERS AND THEIR UNIONS

To speak plain English, the manufacturers are stronger than we are and until we recognize that, we will never succeed...until we can control them at the ballot box.
— President William Cunnane, Cotton Weavers Protective Society

During the fifty years before the 1928 strike, weavers, spinners, loomfixers and the other skilled craftspeople formed separate and usually independent unions. These crafts and their unions were dominated by immigrants from the textile centers of Lancashire and Yorkshire in the north of England. Almost all New Bedford mill workers were immigrants, but only the English and the "Lancaster Irish" (immigrants from the north of England who had left Ireland earlier) brought a strong trade union tradition with them. The successes and failures in New Bedford during the years before the strike tempered this tradition, and the craft unions remained English to their core. The majority of mill workers, mostly French-Canadian, Portuguese, Cape Verdean and Polish immigrants, were not union members by discrimination, choice or because they were working at jobs not covered by the craft unions.

English union leaders found organizing their own an easier task than recruiting workers of different nationalities. The English workers saw the United States as an extension of their home country, having the same language and similar national customs. Although the English-born mill workers had regarded mill owners as enemies in England, in New Bedford they valued the mill owners as fellow Englishmen and allies in the New World. In contrast, they viewed other mill workers as foreigners with different languages and mysterious customs, who appreciated higher wages but didn't have the discipline, perseverance or intelligence necessary to be good union members. Reinforcing these attitudes, the mill owners probably treated workers of their own nationality better than they did other immigrants.

Robert Howard, circa 1890. A union leader in England before he moved to the United States, Howard led the Fall River Spinners Association from 1879 to 1897. He won eight terms in the Massachusetts state senate, where he chaired the labor committee and passed a law reducing the work week to 58 hours.
Fall River Historical Society: Sylvia, Spinner III

Certificate of membership to the National Cotton Mule Spinners Association of America, circa 1870.
Fall River Historical Society

EARLY UNIONS AND THE FIGHT FOR THE TEN-HOUR DAY

The roots of New Bedford's craft unions go back to Fall River and the fight to limit the work day to ten hours.

Beginning in the 1830s, the mostly male workers in Fall River joined with the working women of Lowell in sending the Massachusetts legislature several petitions to reduce the work day to ten hours. Although many legislators spoke in support of the workers, the legislature ruled that the conditions of work were the business of employers and employees and not of the state. Furthermore, they argued that a law restricting the working day would handicap Massachusetts mills in competition with firms from outside the state.[1]

In the 1840s, Fall River's English craftsmen and mechanics tried other strategies to win the ten-hour day. They refused to work more than ten hours a day, arguing to the mill owners that the obligations of family and citizenship required a shorter working day; craftsmen who worked longer than ten hours were forsaking their duties to God, family and community.[2] These better-paid, skilled mechanics also petitioned mill owners directly for the ten-hour day but rarely included other workers in their strategies. Because workers were not united, these tactics failed.

Finally, after 20 years of forging alliances among themselves, Fall River mill workers won the ten-hour day without a cut in pay. Late in 1866, Fall River textile workers formed the Fall River Amalgamated Short Time Committee to petition the owners for a ten-hour day.[3] When the owners refused, the Committee struck and succeeded in closing the mills. After two weeks without production and with State Senator Samuel Chace acting as mediator, Fall River's mill owners accepted the ten-hour day starting on January 1, 1867.

The movement quickly spread to New Bedford, where Thomas Bennett, Jr. agent and founder of the Wamsutta Mills, agreed to cut the work day to ten hours if mill owners throughout New England followed suit. When they didn't, Bennett returned to the old schedule, and the workers threatened to strike. The local clergy and newspapermen, long known for their liberal views on slavery and other forms of oppression but ignorant of the complexities of textile wage rates, offered a compromise of a reduction to ten hours with a proportional cut in pay. Bennett accepted, but the agreement split the workers' unity. Skilled workers, who usually were paid by the piece, could maintain their previous wages by working faster, but unskilled workers, who generally were paid by the week, would have to work for lower wages at the faster pace dictated by the skilled workers. Amidst the dissension between the skilled and unskilled workers over the issue, Bennett fired five leaders of the movement. All workers then walked off the job, demanding that Bennett rehire the strike leaders and continue the ten-hour day without the pay cut.

The strikers succeeded in keeping out strikebreakers and winning community support, and they offered Bennett a three-month trial period of a ten-hour day with no pay cut. If others cities didn't follow, the workers would return to the longer work day. Rachel Howland, a Quaker minister and the city's leading philanthropist, convinced Bennett to accept the offer, but he wouldn't promise to take back the strike leaders. Angered by his refusal to rehire their leaders, a majority of mill workers voted to

Thomas Bennett, Jr., circa 1885.
Bennett built and managed the Wamsutta Mills from its beginning in 1846 until 1874. Bennett directed the company toward the development of quality, fine cotton shirting and sheeting.

Hough

View of the Bennett Mill, circa 1890.
Built in 1889 in what was still a rural North End near Coggeshall Street, this was the city's seventh textile mill. In the lower right corner stands the Workingmen's Club. Founded by English textile workers, the club distributed food throughout the 1928 strike.

Bill Boucher

rescind the offer and continue the strike with the original demands. But the next day most workers returned to the mill under the old conditions, and the strike collapsed.[4]

After Bennett fired all members of the strike committee, the workers' organization disintegrated, but ten years later, in 1877, a similar organization rose in opposition to the third wage cut in three years. After a majority of Wamsutta workers threatened to resign if the wage cut went through, the company retracted the latest cut. Encouraged by this victory, workers voted to strike unless the other wage cuts were also rescinded and speedups reduced. When the company refused, the workers walked out. Although the city's clergy and newspapermen were not as sympathetic to the workers' cause as they had been ten years earlier, William Henry Johnson, an ex-slave who had become a lawyer in the city, served as legal council for the striking workers, and Daniel Ricketson, the town's leading intellectual, chaired a number of the union meetings.[5]

Rachel Howland, circa 1860. A Quaker minister for 55 years, Howland was a board director of the City Mission and of the Association for the Relief of Aged Women.
New Bedford Whaling Museum

An appeal to New England mill workers for strike support during the 1877 strike in New Bedford. It reads, "We hope you will render us the best assistance which lies in your power to do, for we feel confident that should we be defeated it will be a defeat for the whole of the factory operatives in New England."
New Bedford Whaling Museum

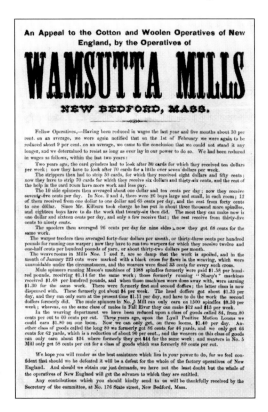

The 1877 strike armed the mill owners with the weapons that would prove decisive 50 years later in the 1928 strike: weak textile markets and ethnic divisions among mill workers. English workers kept to themselves except during hard times, when they sought solidarity with the other mill workers in a strike or other action against wage cuts. But these protests often coincided with weak textile markets, which severely limited the workers' chances for success. The mill owners could sell their inventories of finished cloth into the slow market during a strike and outlast the fragile coalition of mill workers.

In the ten years since the fight for the ten-hour day, the French-Canadian population in the mill had increased but was alienated from the English majority, which held the better jobs. Most of the non-striking workers were French-Canadian. The solidly English strike leaders were forced to pay French Canadians most of the strike relief funds to keep them out of the mills.[6] The strike committee also had French translators at membership meetings. But three months after the strike started, workers began to drift back into the mills. John Smith, president of the strike committee, accused the French-Canadian workers of breaking the strike and blamed the French-Canadian pastor of Sacred Heart Church for advising them to return to work.[7] A few days later, the strike collapsed when most workers accepted the wage cut.

As the number of New Bedford mills rapidly increased over the next 20 years, workers' organizations focused on a single craft slowly took shape. In 1880, the mulespinners, men highly trained in their craft and almost entirely British, were the first to organize.[8] In 1889, they joined with the stronger organization in Fall River to form a national organization within the American Federation of Labor (AFL).[9] Within a few years, weavers, loomfixers and other skilled tradespeople formed their own craft unions in the city. There were several small strikes during this period, usually over an issue specific to a craft in a single mill and sometimes successful.[10]

Mulespinning room at the Potomska Mills, circa 1880. "New Bedford is indebted to Lancashire for more than machinery," wrote English journalist T.M. Young after his 1902 American visit. "In nearly every mill one finds Englishmen in responsible positions—sometimes in supreme charge." In the nineteenth century, New Bedford union members often ended their meetings singing, "God Save the Queen."
Spinner Collection: Young

Prepare for the Great Strike!

Provisions from Boston Beef Co.

How to Live 10 Weeks For $10.

The Boston Beef Co.,
132 Union St.
138 Blackmer St.   937 Acushnet Ave.

Newspaper ad, three days after the 1898 strike began. During the nineteenth century, strikes were an accepted event in community life and a sales opportunity. Later in the strike, Waite & Co. advertised, "No strike here, buy a carpet," and Gifford & Co. offered clothing at strike prices. Another clothier, Swift & Co., announced in bold type, "5% Accepted, An Amicable Settlement by Compromise" when a customer asked for a ten percent price cut.
Evening Standard

THE STRIKE OF 1898

The 1898 strike was a prelude to the 1928 strike. Both were caused by a ten percent wage cut, and in both strikes New Bedford, which was the most profitable New England textile center and had the best organized unions, led the resistance to the wage cuts. Some New Bedford unions had the same leaders in both strikes. In 1898, these leaders were young idealists presiding over a growing industry; in 1928, they were old veterans trying to maintain union power in a declining industry. Remembering the lost 1898 strike and the splits between conservative and socialist ideologies, the conservative craft union leaders were determined to maintain control 30 years later when they faced a similar threat to their leadership.

In December 1897, mill owners throughout New England announced a ten percent wage cut for all textile workers, claiming that increased competition from the South and large inventories of finished cloth forced them to cut costs. Even though New Bedford's mills produced fine cloth not affected by southern competition, the owners of the 18 cotton mills declared themselves in agreement with mill owners in other cities and imposed a wage cut.

Mill workers in other New England centers quietly accepted the wage cut, and by January 1, 1898, all seven craft unions in the Fall River Textile Council had voted against striking.[11] New Bedford's unions were hopeful, however, because the mills were locally owned and because a strike in New Bedford while others were operating would encourage the local mill owners to settle quickly or lose business to their rivals. Also, the New Bedford mill workers looked for financial support from those working under wage cuts elsewhere, because a successful strike would raise everyone's wages.

"The Morning Crowd at the Bristol Mill... The picket of strikers was early on the scene, with note books handy to jot down whatever stragglers chose to brave the displeasure of the crowd... Not more than half a dozen of the help went into the mills, and they were greeted with a shower of frozen dirt and a few tin cans."
Evening Standard

On January 17, the day when the wage cut was to take effect, New Bedford's six thousand union spinners, weavers and loomfixers walked out, with the nine thousand unorganized mill workers joining them. Some craft unions were well-organized, including the mulespinners, who had the largest strike fund in New England. With donations from mill workers in other cities who were not on strike, the New Bedford unions could afford to pay their members enough to survive for at least a few weeks. And although they had become less generous over the years, the Overseers of the Poor still paid about one-third of the average mill worker's wage to strikers. State law limited this payment to eight weeks, however.[12]

Even before the pay cut went into effect, most newspapers in New Bedford and elsewhere supported the workers in their struggle. The *Boston Sunday Post* printed a story comparing the $750 weekly salary of Andrew Pierce, a mill official, with the $3 weekly pay of a typical mill worker.[13] Even the conservative *Boston Herald* hinted that the largest mills in New Bedford were mismanaged and called for an outside audit of the mills' books.[14] The major New York newspapers sent reporters to New Bedford, who concluded that New Bedford workers were impoverished before the pay cut. Joseph Pulitzer's *New York World* compared the living conditions of mill workers to slaves and concluded that slaves had lived better.[15]

They have said that the textile industries of the South are growing to such proportions and that the wages in the South are so much lower and the hours so much longer that they can't compete with them. Nothing is further from the truth than such a claim. I will not deny that the wages are lower and the hours are longer than eastern operatives', but there never yet was an industry permanently successfully conducted upon the basis of low wages and long hours of labor. I call your attention to all countries and you will

Andrew G. Pierce, owner of several mills and president of the Cotton Manufacturers' Association.

Hough

"Crowd at Bristol Mill at 6PM Monday... *Superintendent Law with his clerk left the mill office by the entrance on Coggeshall Street and was escorted through Coggeshall Street to Acushnet Avenue by the police.*"

Evening Standard

Charles Ashley, Frank Milliken and Samuel Ross. *Young men on the rise in 1898: Ashley as mayor, Milliken as district court judge and Ross as mulespinners' president and state representative. All three played the same roles in 1928, except that Ross no longer was in the state legislature.*
Standard-Times, New Bedford Free Public Library

find that wherever the hours of labor are least and the wages higher, there you will find the most progressive people and the industries most successful. You may go where you please, it doesn't matter, you will find that this is the absolute rule. If low wages meant industrial and commercial progress, then China ought to stand at the head of civilization.

— Samuel Gompers[16]

The mill owners ignored the bad press. Backed by large inventories of unsold cloth and bound together by family and business ties, they maintained the pay cut. When union leaders requested direct negotiations with the mill owners through Mayor Charles S. Ashley, former member of the Knights of Labor, the mill owners refused. Instead, they demanded that Ashley provide police protection to open the mill gates and enforce a U.S. Supreme Court decision that outlawed picketing outside mill gates.[17] City agencies and the courts eventually lined up behind the mill owners. The Overseers of the Poor stated that anyone accepting aid would be considered a pauper and would not be allowed to vote. Judge Frank Milliken ruled that everyone outside the mill, whether picketing or not, was liable to a fine of $300, roughly equivalent to one year's wages.[18]

Harriet Pickering, a weaver, led a futile attempt to extend union privileges to more workers and strengthen the bonds between mill workers:

If we are to fight a combine, we must do it with a combine. The manufacturers are all combined. Even here in New Bedford when we want to deal with them, we find them united and deal with them in a body. Yet on our side they treat us as the weavers' union and the spinners' union and the card room union. There is no body of the operatives, except when we have a strike on our hands, and that is only for a temporary convention. What I hope to live to see is an amalgamated textile union, embodying everything.[19]

There also were conflicts among the craft unions. The weavers union, the city's largest, tried to introduce other issues besides the wage cut into the conflict. The weavers especially resented being fined for imperfect cloth, which they claimed was caused by substandard material they received from workers earlier in the production process. Other craft workers weren't concerned about fines and bristled at the weavers' suggestion of their incompetence.

Harriet Pickering. *A weaver who criticized local union leaders for their narrow concerns, Pickering wasn't allowed the use of a hall by the union executive committee for a meeting of women weavers. She often was greeted with derision when she tried to speak at union meetings. She died in the hospital for the insane at Worcester.*
Ashley Scrapbook

Eugene Debs, Daniel DeLeon and Samuel Gompers. Each was a leader of a political faction of the U.S. labor movement at the turn of the century, and each gave fiery speeches in New Bedford in 1898. DeLeon made his most important speech there, explaining his theory of socialism: "The truth of it is that instead of the wage earner being supported by the capitalist, it is the capitalist who is supported by the wage worker."

Standard-Times, Ashley Scrapbook

The conflict in the labor movement between conservative and socialist political ideologies caused a more serious split among the craft union members. Samuel Gompers, who had founded the AFL in 1886 and served as its president until his death in 1924, favored craft organizations of skilled workmen, focusing strictly on wages and working conditions for their members. He strongly opposed the political activity of the various socialist parties. The socialists, led by Daniel DeLeon and Eugene Debs, sought broader goals for a unified working class, including higher income, better working conditions for all, and ultimately workers' control of mills and factories.

At the height of the strike, Gompers visited the city to recruit members for the AFL because only the mulespinners and the carders unions belonged to his group.[20] At an open meeting, union members in the audience who supported more militant tactics and socialist goals criticized Gompers over the narrowness of the AFL's goals. He responded by calling DeLeon a spy for the mill owners.[21]

> *Men who will not fight together are traitors to each other. I am tolerant of difference of opinion. I am willing that everybody should have a hearing as any man should, but in the face of a battle no division can be tolerated.*
> — Samuel Gompers[22]

DeLeon, never one to miss a fight, came to New Bedford after Gompers had left and publicly scolded him for abandoning the majority of mill workers, calling him "a labor fakir."[23] Eugene Debs, later to win almost one million votes as the Socialist candidate for President, then came to the city and tried to smooth the waters, calling for unity against the mill owners during the strike.[24]

For the majority of strikers, the main issue was relief funds. Even though they had collected money from union and non-union textile workers throughout New England, the craft unions paid strike relief only to their members. When the lower-paid mill workers, many of whom had been excluded from the unions, demanded a share of these relief funds, the craft unions dropped some of their restrictions for membership and allowed new members to collect strike pay. But the slowing trickle of donations could not cover the wider distribution, and all looked to Gompers and the AFL for relief, because the socialist parties had little money to offer.

"Mrs. Pickering Rises to Ask a Question." Harriet Pickering often criticized local union leaders, but she wouldn't allow DeLeon to attack Ross as a "labor fakir." When DeLeon spoke in New Bedford, she rose from her seat, "her face white as a sheet," and asked DeLeon if he thought that Ross was working for the mill owners. DeLeon was forced to say no.

Evening Standard

William Cunnane, president of the Weavers Protection Association and secretary of the strike council in 1898. Cunnane was a socialist who believed that unions should form a political party and concentrate on political power. Other council members followed Gompers' strategy of political neutrality.

Standard-Times

Women mill workers waiting for their pay. Boston and New York newspapers sympathized with the low pay and harsh working conditions in textile mills. A New York World reporter found the strikers hungry and pale, having a "waxy whiteness which was frightening."

Boston Post, Ashley Scrapbook: New York World

Hopes were raised when Gompers returned to the city. But Gompers concentrated on his differences with DeLeon, calling him a "sneaking wolf," and didn't pledge any strike relief from the AFL.[25] Samuel Ross, the president of the mulespinners and the AFL's staunchest supporter in New Bedford, dismissed the widely held hope that the AFL would supply more relief funds, saying, "There was never any foundation for it except in the imagination of the newspaper reporters."[26]

After three months on strike, the mill workers were destitute. Strike funds and public relief had run out long before. Tenement owners, pushed by the city's demand for back taxes and payment for city services, began evicting workers, and the Wamsutta evicted striking workers from their mill-owned housing. The newspapers also reported that retail grocers throughout the city no longer would offer groceries on credit. Many striking mill workers were starving, and some were homeless.

Seeing their chance, some mill owners publicly claimed that the proposed cut was not ten percent but ranged from three to ten percent. Union leaders grasped this straw as grounds for a settlement and offered a compromise five percent pay cut. However, the strike was broken when the mill owners refused this compromise and announced they were opening their gates to start up the mills. Mayor Ashley supplied local and state police to guard the mill gates, and agents for the Overseers of the

Poor insured that those who had received relief "grasped the chance to support themselves."[27] As the workers began drifting back to work, the city's newspapers publicized the increasing numbers of people returning to work and pronounced the strike over. One by one the unions surrendered, and union and non-union workers straggled back to work, taking whatever wages and working conditions management offered.

THE TEXTILE COUNCIL RISES FROM DEFEAT

In 1898, the conservative leaders within the Textile Council, a federation of local textile craft unions founded a few years earlier, faced opposition within their own ranks from more militant union leaders. Towards the strike's end the conservatives gained the upper hand when they forced William Cunnane, the president of the weavers union and the Council's leading socialist, to resign as strike committee secretary.[28] Afterwards, the Council turned increasingly toward a narrow vision of better wages and working conditions for its members.

In the years following the strike, the Council healed the splits between unions as English workers made places for their own in the mills, in unions and in politics. Strong demand for finely woven cotton cloth helped make this strategy a success, because both union and non-union workers gained, if unevenly, from the increased demand for labor. During the decade after the strike, New Bedford's mill owners built 12 new mills in the city. While most coarse cloth production moved to the South, New Bedford consolidated its rule over the fine cloth market, aided by a high tariff on foreign products.

Overproduction, 1898. A poem by William Cunnane under his nom de plume, Tucker.

There's too much wheat on the prairie
  Then why don't the starving eat
Too much beef on the hillsides,
  But we ain't stalled with meat.
Too much cloth in the factories,
  He shook the leg of his ragged pants
Shirts and hose and draperies
  And all that the people want
Too much of all but confidence
  Then tell me the reason why
If starving folks got the means to
  Why then don't they buy

Workers at Wamsutta Mills head home after work on a Saturday afternoon in the spring of 1898 after the strike ended.
Spinner Collection

The number of mill workers in New Bedford doubled in this period, mostly from Portuguese immigration, but the English mill workers maintained their tight hold on union leadership and skilled jobs. French Canadians held most of the remaining skilled jobs. Although one-half of the mill workers were Portuguese or Cape Verdean, in 1926 they held less than ten percent of the skilled jobs.[29]

As a matter of fact, their whole group was made up primarily of Anglo-Saxons. They had the better jobs and the whole relationship in the plant was that you got a job through the foreman, and the foreman kept the better jobs for the elite, which were the Anglo-Saxons. And that's the way it worked.
— Jack Rubenstein

The slavery department of a cotton mill was the card room. You never sat down. You always had plenty of work to do and were never paid much money. Mostly Portuguese and Cape Verdean people worked there. They would never hire a colored guy and put him in the spinning room. They would never make a weaver out of him. Not that the white guys wouldn't work with him. We'd have been glad to. It was management's way of doing things. The management kept us apart. The management kept the colored people in the card room. You saw very few white people in there, except for the boss.
— Pete Fauteux

Men and boys in the Grinnell Mill, circa 1900. Weaving, mulespinning and loomfixing were the skilled professions in a cotton mill, performed mostly by men from Lancashire, England. T.M. Young met a weaver, "a Darwen man," in the Granite Mills in Fall River. "'This is the right side of the water,' he cried into my ear through the din of the looms. 'Do you mean better to live in?' I replied. 'No,' was the answer, 'better for making money. I would sooner live in England, and if I can save enough to keep me out of the mill, I'll go home before I die.'"

Spinner Collection: Young

Weave room of the Hathaway Mill, circa 1910. Women worked at yarn-related jobs such as ring spinning, spooling, warp tending and doffing. The women pictured here, though flanked by weavers, are probably ring spinners, as evidenced by the tools strapped around their waists. Second from right is 16-year-old Mary Jeffrey.
Spinner Collection

Early in the twentieth century, the Textile Council often elected members to city and state positions. Samuel Ross was elected to the state legislature for over 20 years, first as a state representative and then as a state senator.[30] John Halliwell, a secretary of the carders union, also was elected as a state representative and senator, serving in the legislature during the 1928 strike.[31] In 1918, the English workers formed the Labor Party. In 1919, Arthur Harriman, their candidate for mayor, lost by less than five percent of the vote, and the Labor Party managed to capture one-half of the Common Council.[32]

Although working-class candidates of English descent continued to win local elections, 1919 proved the highwater mark for the Labor party. In 1920, in a campaign in which labor was portrayed as a special interest, Harriman lost badly to Ashley, and few Labor candidates were elected to the Common Council. The party split in 1922, and in 1923 the Labor party lost all its seats on the Common Council.

Following their success in gaining skilled jobs, French Canadians also did well in city politics. Between 1912 and 1930, about 20 percent of city aldermen and ten percent of Common Council members were French-Canadian.[33] The Portuguese did not share in these political successes, however. During the same period, no Portuguese aldermen were elected, and only six percent of the Common Council members were Portuguese.[34] French-Canadian and British voters probably supported each other in elections, keeping out the Portuguese candidates. The Portuguese, alienated in the mills, in unions and in political life, also were less likely to become citizens.

Conservative leadership in the Textile Council firmly held power by 1901, when New Bedford's textile unions joined with those in Fall River and elsewhere to form the United Textile Workers (UTW), an affiliate of the AFL under the leadership of John Golden of Fall River. But the city's craft unions resisted the national association, opposing Golden's use of their dues to build a stronger national union.[35] With a solid English mistrust of anything foreign, the New Bedford and Fall River craft unions were reluctant to tax themselves to support textile workers elsewhere. By 1916, all local craft unions in Fall River and New Bedford had left the UTW to form the National Amalgamation of Textile Operators. Eventually the group became the American Federation of Textile Operatives (AFTO), a weak national organization with low per capita dues.[36]

More militant unions like the Industrial Workers of the World (IWW) failed to make any headway in the city. In 1912, fresh from its victory in the bitter "Bread and Roses" strike in Lawrence, the IWW tried to interest New Bedford's mill workers in a strike over working conditions. The organization attracted only a few hundred members and was isolated by the established union leaders, who actively opposed the IWW's goals and tactics.[37]

Labor party ticket, New Bedford, 1920. The Labor Party was formed in New Bedford after World War 1. In 1919, Labor candidate Arthur Harriman lost to Mayor Ashley by less than 500 votes, and the Labor party won half the seats on the Common Council. In 1920, however, Harriman lost to Ashley by over five thousand votes. There had been a split in the Labor ticket, and women, who voted for the first time in 1920, generally voted against Labor.

Clark, Evening Standard

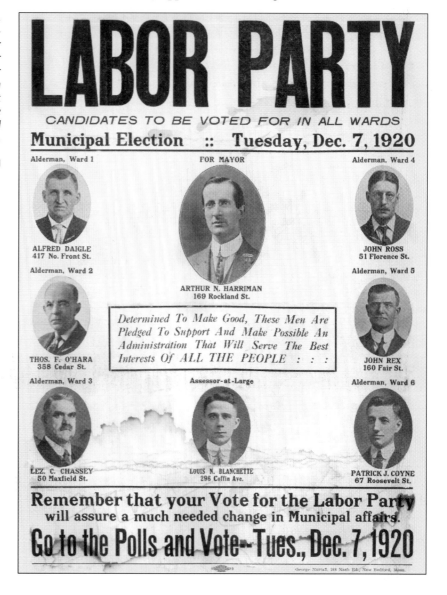

Members of the Fall River loomfixers; Union members enjoy the Labor Day festivities at their union hall on 370 Bedford Street in 1903.

Fall River Historical Society

THE GREAT WAR AND THE ROARING '20s

The textile industry boomed during World War I as it had in previous wars. This war of attrition between immense armies called for ever-increasing amounts of textiles for bandages, uniforms, blankets, airplane covering and cotton tire cord. Production and profits in textile manufacture rose sharply. In the North, a stagnant industry was given a new lease on life as mill owners sped up the pace, trying to squeeze more profit from outdated machinery. Mill owners in the South, confident of their future in textiles and encouraged by wartime demand, built new mills and operated around the clock.

New Bedford was especially well suited to take advantage of this boom. Parachutes, airplane covering, and tire cord required combing, a process New Bedford mills had developed in manufacturing fine cloth. Before the war, the city's mills concentrated on finely woven cloth, but profits from war materials were too high to ignore, and New Bedford's textile industry switched to coarsely woven products for the military.[38]

During the war years, sales more than quadrupled, and profits increased sixfold.[39] Labor shared in the wartime boom. Five thousand more people were employed in the mills, where the average wage more than doubled.[40] New Bedford's population had tripled in three decades to 100,000, and the city's commerce flourished on a diet of full employment and higher wages.

State Pier, 1918. During the boom years of World War I, New Bedford built the State Pier to deliver cotton directly to its port, replacing the rail link to New York. In 1918, New Bedford mills consumed two million bales of cotton, or 265 shiploads, and the new pier soon was too small for the textile traffic. Today the State Pier is a maritime terminal.

New Bedford Free Public Library: Boss, Thomas

Weave room of the Nashawena Mills, circa 1920. The Nashawena boasted having the world's largest weave room, with floor space of six acres, housing over four thousand looms, all under a single roof. "Practically every known useful variety and size of loom is represented in the equipment of this mill," stated its advertising agents. "Tell us what you want, and we can make it."

Spinner Collection: Whitman

The Textile Council fought for a share of the immense wartime profits. When the mill owners, encouraged by the federal government, offered a 15 percent raise late in 1918, the Council demanded 25 percent. the Council remained unmoved by the mill owners' appeals to patriotism and staged a two-day strike to gain a small increase over the mill owners' offer.[41]

Wartime prosperity wasn't based on a permanent foundation, however. During the war, New Bedford mill owners directed their production toward military sales. When the war ended, demand for military products dropped, and the mills began accumulating unsold cloth rather than profits.

Like their fathers and grandfathers, the mill owners, mindful of the long, slow decline of whaling 50 years earlier, cautiously began withdrawing from textile production. Although most of their equipment was old and

outdated, they didn't invest their profits in new textile machinery. When Henry Ford was searching for textile machinery for his museum, he came to New Bedford and took running equipment from the floor of the Grinnell Mill.

The Textile Council didn't give in easily. During the spring of 1920, eleven of the 13 unions in New Bedford voted to join the loomfixers in a strike calling for a wage increase, but the underlying issues were work rules; the loomfixers had been forced to work without helpers. The unions claimed to represent over half of New Bedford's textile workers and, encouraged by the pattern set during the war, expected a quickly negotiated settlement. The mill owners, tired of wartime concessions, proved the unions wrong. They refused to negotiate, claiming that the unions were influenced by radical elements and were trying to establish a "soviet system."[42] The unions quickly learned that the days of easy victories and rising wages were over. After Mayor Ashley failed to bring the owners to the bargaining table, a short, weakly supported strike forced union leaders to cave in. The few mill workers who remained on strike straggled back to work.

In the fall of 1920, the cloth market collapsed and the mill workers' situation deteriorated further. The owners laid off thousands of mill workers, and production trickled to a stop. The Cotton Manufacturers' Association, representing New Bedford's cotton mill owners, asked for a 30 percent wage cut to take effect in December, when they planned to reopen the mills. The Textile Council objected but was powerless because almost all the city's textile workers were out of work. Abraham Binns, the Council's president and head of the weavers union, called unsuccessfully for a Congressional inquiry into the wage reduction. Binns, as a member of the Overseers of the Poor, also begged for more relief funds. When the mills reopened in February 1921, mill workers were forced to accept a 20 percent wage cut.

Jacquard looms at the Nashawena Mills, circa 1929. The weaver on the Jacquard used a complex punched-card system to produce the most intricate weaves. The agents of the Nashawena praised the weavers' skill: "A roomful of looms cannot make good cloth by themselves. Machinery has no intelligence and no conscience. Human skill and alertness have become more important than ever."

Whitman

View from a downtown bank building looking toward the South End, circa 1920. From here, the stacks of mills along the waterfront include glass works, tool and dye manufacturing, the gas company and textile mills. New Bedford's industrial strength peaked during this period.

New Bedford Free Public Library

A carding machine operator at Wamsutta Mills feeds raw cotton into the hopper where it is pulled apart or "carded" on the revolving spiked apron of the carder.
Standard-Times

In those days they could cut you just like that. You could leave Friday, go in Monday, and there would be a notice that stated that as of that week your pay would be cut ten percent. It was as simple as that. And if they gave you the ten percent back you always lost a dime anyway.

— Vic Marginson

By the end of 1921, textile wages in New Bedford had fallen by more than one-third from their high in 1920, and wages fell another 15 percent over the next six years.[43] By 1927, average yearly earnings for New Bedford mill workers had fallen to about $1,000 ($7,000 at today's prices), less than one-half of the U.S. government estimate for a "minimum health and decency budget."

Alfred Severs, Joseph Figueiredo and Al Saulnier remembered the hard times in New Bedford's mills during the 1920s:

It was my job as a youngster to bring my father his dinner. I would go into the mill, into where my father worked, bringing him the dinner pail. There was this great big bay where all this loose soft cotton was. And they would just lie down in this big cotton bin and have their dinner. People complain today about air pollution, but it's nothing compared to the air pollution that existed in some of the areas where people worked. Of course there were other problems in the mills too. There was sound pollution. You talk about air pollution — there was sound pollution inside the mills.

— Alfred Severs

The women working in the mills were also raising families. You would look at their faces, and they were faces of people that were worn out. Many

"Jo Benevides, Curled Up in a Doffing Box, Eating his Lunch, 1912." At this time, 14 was supposed to be the minimum working age. Hine, however, found that children as young as nine were allowed to work by using false identification supplied by their parents or by simply lying about their age.

Lewis W. Hine

of them had large families, and they had to take care of their children, take care of their family life. They thought of themselves last.

— Joe Figueiredo

My father went broke. We were 21 in my family. No, that's right. No twins. And we always had fresh food on our table for years and years. I never knew how we got it until I was about 16 years old. My father used to go down and pick up all the fruit for the pigs. We cleaned up all the bad stuff. We'd wash it all off and it was only a small cup, but we had fresh fruit. We ate well!

— Al Saulnier

But compared to the rest of the New England textile industry, New Bedford was a bright spot. In 1922, cooperation between the mill owners and the Textile Council helped New Bedford avoid the wage cuts and ferocious strikes that raged throughout the South and the rest of New England. The strikes in Pawtucket, Manchester, Lawrence, Fitchburg and other cities broke their local unions. National membership in the UTW fell from 80,000 in 1920 to 15,000 in 1922.[44] Everywhere except in New Bedford, mill owners had eliminated unions by cutting wages, demanding concessions and forcing strikes.

New Bedford's turn would come in 1928.

Young French-Canadian women in the warping room at the Whitman Mill, 1910. Standing at left is 16-year-old Bernadette Desmarais.

Gift of Roland Jodoin

Well, as I say, sometimes the
boss does the organizing for you.

– Frank Manning

ANNOUNCEMENT

Operating costs in the cotton mills of New England have undergone such changes that New Bedford manufacturers are confronted with a situation which is not only abnormal but extremely critical.

Lower Wages in Other Localities

In many of the cotton mills of New England wage reductions have become effective. The operatives in New Bedford cotton mills now receive wages that are much higher than what is paid for the same class of work in competing mills elsewhere. Some of these mills can operate 54 hours per week. In addition, there are no legal restrictions as to night work for female operatives, which is an advantage in getting out orders for quick deliveries.

New Bedford Handicapped

It should be obvious that New Bedford manufacturers, paying the old wage scale, limited to a 48-hour week and restricted as to night work, must be doing business under a serious handicap.

Competition

New Bedford cotton mills have been struggling under these unfair conditions for a long time. It is now essential that they get their production costs nearer those of their competitors if they are to continue in operation.

Reluctant to Reduce Wages

When, in other sections of New England, cotton manufacturers reduced wages, New Bedford cotton mills refrained from taking similar action. Various plans were considered which it was hoped might relieve the situation without affecting the earnings of the operatives. Unfortunately, none of these solves the problem.

Owing to the competitive conditions which exist, New Bedford mills are forced to make a reduction in wages of 10 per cent, effective Monday, April 16th, 1928, and have posted notices accordingly in the mills named below.

It is hoped this will relieve the situation sufficiently to enable local corporatons to take orders which would otherwise go to competitors.

Acushnet Mill Corp.	Holmes Mfg. Co.	Pierce Bros. Ltd.
Beacon Mfg. Co.	Kilburn Mills	Pierce Mfg. Corp.
Booth Mfg. Co.	Nashawena Mills Co.	Potomska Mills Corp.
Bristol Mfg. Corp.	Neild Mfg. Corp.	Quissett Mill
Butler Mills	N. B. Cotton Mills Corp.	Sharp Mfg. Co.
City Mfg. Corp.	N. B. Spinning Co.	Soule Mill
Gosnold Mills Co.	Nonquitt Spinning Co	Taber Mill, Inc.
Grinnell Mfg. Corp.	Page Mfg. Co.	Wamsutta Mills
Hathaway Mfg. Co.	Pemaquid Mills	Whitman Mills

The wage cut announcement appeared on Easter Monday, 1928 [*Ashley Scrapbook*]

CHAPTER 3

THE STRIKE BEGINS

I just turned 17. It was after Easter. We had our Easter holiday and had gone back to work, and a notice was on the board saying that the following week we would work at a ten percent cut in our wages. That caused a lot of excitement, and the superintendent explained to us that they had gone to New York and could not renew their orders at the price that they formerly had paid. Consequently, we should work at a ten percent cut. Well, in those days we were not totally unionized. But nevertheless, after some meetings they decided that they would go on strike. Well, naturally the whole mill shut down. There was no need for a cloth inspector if there were no weavers weaving cloth.

– Gladys Howcroft, cloth inspector

The mill owners' announcement of a ten percent wage cut on Monday, April 9, 1928, angered workers and directly challenged the leaders of the Textile Council.[1] After the strike of 1898, the city's mill owners had promised to give the Textile Council 30 days notice before cutting wages.[2] Since then, the Textile Council slowly had emerged as partners with management in production, and the mill owners consulted with them over wages and working conditions. The city's craft unions had won respect from the media, built contacts with the business community and elected members to the state legislature and local government. But their success always rested on the sandy foundation of the majority of textile workers who were not union members.

Few labor leaders in the city were eager to contest the mill owners. Some, like Samuel Ross of the mulespinners, remembered the owners' show of strength in 1898. But they had little choice. After 30 years of more or less peaceful accommodation, the Textile Council leaders purposely had been insulted and their authority had been threatened when the mill owners ignored them in announcing the wage cut. Abraham Binns, president of the weavers union and treasurer of the Council, called the wage cut "an indefensible exhibition of savagery, coming as it does after seven years of layoffs and wage cuts."[3]

Cartoons from the Evening Standard.
New Bedford's three newspapers strongly criticized New Bedford's mills for not advertising, for not following fashions and for nepotism. The city's newspapers blamed the mill owners for causing the strike by cutting wages. As the strike grew longer, the newspapers weakened in their support for restoring the wage cut but continued to criticize the mill owners for out-of-date business practices.

Ashley Scrapbook

CITIZENS DEBATE THE WAGE CUT

The Textile Council found allies among the city's clergy, who argued that the wage cut was unfair because mill wages were already below the poverty level. Most of the mill owners lived in the city, where their wealth and luxury contrasted sharply with the low wages and deprivation of mill workers and their families. Wealth and poverty seemed different sides of the same coin; great wealth for a few seemed to result from low wages for the majority. Aside from the financial community, most of New Bedford's population had little love for the mill owners.

The mill owners were making a lot of money but they were obviously never satisfied, no matter how much they made. They always wanted to make more, and the way they did it was by taking it off the hides of the workers by increasing their production with less workers. This was called speedup in which they would speed the operation of the various machines and increase their workload. The workers used to resist it.

— Joe Figueiredo

The city's merchants, who always had been strongly influenced by their clergy, agreed. They also realized that lower wages would depress the local economy. Over 80 percent of the city's working population was employed in the manufacture of cotton textiles. Mill workers filled the city's churches and spent their wages in local stores.

Nor could the mill owners count on the media for support. A typical editorial at the beginning of the strike said of the mill owners, "Among the newspapers of their own city, they could not find a single editorial comment in their favor."[4] Most local advertising came from the city's merchants, whereas almost none came from the mills because cloth produced in New Bedford was sold not locally but in New York and other commercial centers.

The mill owners countered that competition had forced their hand.[5] They pointed to the general ten percent wage cut that began in Lawrence late in 1927 and quickly spread through Maine and New Hampshire.[6] In January of 1928, the Fall River mill owners had announced a ten percent wage cut to their workers. The mill workers grumbled but their unions, critically weakened by the disastrous strike of 1904–1905 and by competition from the South, weren't strong enough to resist.[7] Fall River union leaders threatened to strike, but on January 28, 1928, a strike vote failed to carry. Although the majority of union members wanted to strike, the motion fell 11 votes short of the required two–thirds majority. On January 30, 1928, the pay cut quietly went into effect in Fall River.[8]

Although New Bedford had suffered a recession in 1926, most mills had recouped their losses in 1927. In that year, profits for the New Bedford mills exceeded $2.5 million and stock prices, which had fallen to their lowest levels in 20 years, were beginning to recover. Furthermore, competition for textile workers in the city, which normally would raise wages not reduce them, had increased. By 1928, three major tire companies — Firestone, Goodyear and Fiske — had located large plants in New Bedford which employed three thousand mill workers to manufacture cotton tire cord, the fabric used in tires. (Steel and nylon replaced cotton during the 1960s.) America's love affair with the auto bloomed during the 1920s. The cotton ply tires that carried it required a toughness and durability perfected in New Bedford during 50 years of producing combed cotton yarn.

Problems loomed in New Bedford, however. Late in 1927, overproduction of fine and coarse goods in both southern and northern mills reduced wholesale prices of cotton cloth to critically low levels. In the past, the Manufacturers' Association had responded to soft markets with agreements to curtail production. Unfortunately for the mill owners, the cartel was beginning to come apart at the seams. Some of the less profitable mills saw their survival threatened by a lengthy curtailment; they were not solvent enough to sustain even the temporary loss in revenue that the larger mills easily could withstand. Furthermore, some mill owners were

Interior of Goodyear Mill, 1929.
"When I was a kid, there was the overseer and you couldn't speak to him. He was way up. The second hands, yes, you could talk with them a little. But the only ones who could speak with the overseer were the second hands. Then the superintendent, oh my God, he was on a throne somewhere, you know. And then the agent, he was God, he was like the President of the United States."
Spinner Collection: Isherwood

unable to resist the higher profits from producing cloth when others didn't. Any recovery in prices due to reduced production encouraged members of the cartel to break the agreement and increase their own production. When a 20 percent curtailment was implemented in January 1928, many members did not go along. The result was an overall increase in textile production, further worsening market conditions. When voluntary curtailment failed, a wage cut severe enough to cause a strike could affect the same result as a curtailment.

> *They were making a profit at the time but there was evidently a dip and the mill owners decided that they were going to operate at the same rate of profit even though they were not operating at the same rate of production.*
> - Jack Rubenstein

A wage cut wouldn't directly solve the overproduction problem. Lower wages would mean higher profits, thus encouraging more production. But the mill owners probably expected mill workers and their unions to respond to a pay cut with a general strike as they had in 1898. The owners welcomed a halt in production that they could blame on someone other than themselves. In the meantime, the mills could reduce costs, sell off their stockpiles, and settle the strike in the fall when market conditions traditionally improved.

Weave room of the Nashawena Mill, 1927. During the early 1920s, many of the New Bedford mills had expanded their shares by issuing stock dividends. This would have presented little problem if sales and profits had continued to climb. But by 1926 the pie was shrinking and markets were in decline. In 1927, stocks at the majority of New Bedford mills declined to their lowest prices in 25 years.
New Bedford Free Public Library

Weave room of the Nashawena, 1928.
With stock prices low in 1927, Wall Street brokers began touting the mill stocks as investor bargains. The strategy was successful because mill profits partially recovered in 1927, mainly due to an increase in production. By the end of 1927, prices began falling and overproduction became a problem for the city's mill owners.
Spinner Collection

A strike also would help the financially stronger mills buy out the weaker ones. During the early 1920s, many New Bedford mills had increased their shares by issuing stock dividends. In 1922 alone, the mills increased shares of stock from 33 percent to 200 percent.[9] This increase in total stock outstanding came with an obligation to pay cash dividends on more shares. The mills could afford the increase in total dividends if sales and profit continued to climb, but demand had fallen. By 1927, many of the mills stopped paying dividends altogether, and the average dividend of four percent was the lowest in 25 years. The more powerful mill owners knew that many of their competitors were experiencing financial difficulty and some were approaching bankruptcy. A few bankruptcies of the weaker firms would help the stronger firms consolidate the industry and return to higher profits.

Interlocking directorate in New Bedford, 1928. A few families in the city controlled many of the mills, banks and community organizations. Walter Langshaw, a mill owner but an outsider, wrote, "Four families constitute an oligarchy that disregards the spirit of our constitution."
Ashley Scrapbook

Prominent New Bedford Families on Bank, Mill and other Board Directorates

Andrew G. Pierce, Jr. & Edward T. Pierce (brothers)	James E. Stanton & James E. Stanton, Jr. (son)	Oliver Prescott	John Duff & sons John Jr. and Mark Duff
N.B. Five Cents Savings	Merchants National Bank	N.B. Institution for Savings	N.B. Institution for Savings
First National Bank	Acushnet Mills	First National Bank	Merchants National
N.B. Institution for Savings	Hathaway Mills	Wamsutta Mills	Soule Mill
Pierce Brothers, Ltd.	City Mfg. Co.	Potomska Mills	Sharp Mill
Grinnell Mfg.	New Bedford Cotton Waste Company	Gosnold Mill	Potomska Mills
Pierce Mfg. Corp.	St. Lukes Hospital	New England Gas & Light	Community Welfare Fund
New Bedford Cotton Waste Company	New Bedford Hotel	Morse Twist Drill	Morse Twist Drill
Pairpoint Corp.	Pairpoint Corp.	Union Street Railway	Union Street Railway
Wamsutta Club	Union Street Railway	Pairpoint Corp.	Pairpoint Corp.
New Bedford Opera House	Morse Twist Drill	St. Lukes Hospital	St. Lukes Hospital
Union Street Railway	War Fund Assn.	Swain School	
Morse Twist Drill		Community Welfare Fund	

Local bankers agreed with the strategy of consolidation. They also knew the weaker mills couldn't survive the loss in production from a strike, especially one that dragged on for months. Every New Bedford bank had a few mill owners on its board of directors, which controlled the bank's loan and acquisition policies. Some of the more powerful mill owners sat on several boards, and the bankers had to pay attention to their wishes.

In 1927, Sanford & Kelly, the leading stockbrokers in Fall River and New Bedford, reported, "Several large banking interests are on the lookout to acquire controlling interests in some of the less successful fine goods plants. The purpose for this is to consolidate in the future with other units." Mill stock prices were low and a strike would drive them lower, making buyouts easier.

TEXTILE COUNCIL VOTES TO STRIKE

Between Monday's announcement of the pay cut and the following Monday when it was to take effect, William E. G. Batty, leader of the Textile Council, pressed for a strike vote. Batty was the youngest of New Bedford's labor leaders. Born in England and educated as a young man for missionary work, he became an officer in the Salvation Army. When this didn't suit him, he went into the textile mills, working as a weaver and loomfixer. In 1920, at the age of 30, he became secretary of the loomfixers union and two years later was elected secretary of the Textile Council.

Batty was an energetic organizer and a forceful speaker. Although his union wasn't in the major national union, Batty was becoming a force in national textile organization. He travelled throughout the Northeast, offering New Bedford's help to striking textile workers.

William Evert Gladstone Batty, at the time of the strike. Named for the English prime minister Gladstone, "Here was a man with strong feelings of right and wrong in the treatment of people in their work. And I think he was naturally drawn to it on that account."

Standard-Times: Batty

He was born in Lancashire, England, and came here as a boy. He worked in the textile mills as a loomfixer. Part of the time he was what they called a third hand. But he had a thirst for knowledge and studied even while he was working. He had a scientific approach to his job and kept his job under control so that in the bottom drawer of his tool bench were books.

— Harry Batty

My father was admired by both management and labor. He was fair with both.

— Isabelle Batty Milotte

Batty and the other union chiefs believed that the unorganized textile workers would follow union members out on strike.[10] Even if many didn't, the mills couldn't operate without the skilled union workers, and the Textile Council hoped to completely close down the mills in the Manufacturers' Association. The craft unions had used this strategy in previous strikes against individual mills, usually negotiating terms only for their craft. The Textile Council wouldn't strike against the mills that didn't cut wages. Their goal was to apply competitive pressure to the wage-cutting mills and to keep some money coming into workers' pockets.

None of them led ostentatious lives. Batty didn't. Very simple lives, not like some of the modern labor leaders who travel in limos. None of them had the resources there. It was a local union with no national treasury to draw from, and they were not affiliated with anybody.

– Frank Manning

On Thursday, four days before the wage cut was to take effect and a few hours before the union members were scheduled to vote, Mayor Charles Ashley called for calm and asked the Manufacturers' Association to delay the wage cut by one week. Mayor Ashley, the son of a prominent carriage maker and the owner of a small meat market, had been New Bedford's mayor for over 30 years. Ashley had tried to restore wage cuts in the past. He was unsuccessful in 1898 and 1920, but probably played a role in convincing the Manufacturers' Association to not cut wages in 1922. Ashley never took any direct action against the mill owners, however. In his years as mayor, he had expanded into real estate and other businesses, owing much of his success to the mill owners. In 1920, when he claimed that his office as mayor kept him so busy that his business interests had suffered, the mill owners held a dinner at the Wamsutta Club and presented Ashley with a check for $20,000 (about $150,000 at today's prices) to cover any business losses he incurred as mayor.

Mayor Charles Ashley at his desk. *Ashley was well versed in politics and comfortable with his power. Although he had the support of the mill owners, Ashley called himself "a man of the people."*
Standard-Times

"Pleading with Ashley to Run Again," *1932. The mayor's popularity with the city's business leaders is evident in this photograph "with a group of 50 leaders in the city's business life" urging him to make another election bid. Among those present are mill owners John Duff, seated to the mayor's right, and James E. Stanton, Jr., seated left. Other mill directors present are Henry H. Crapo, Abbot P. Smith, Thomas F. Glennon and William E. Parker. The 73-year-old Ashley did run, and win, again. Between 1890-1937, he served as mayor for 33 years.*
Standard-Times

The Manufacturers' Association agreed to Ashley's proposal to delay the wage cut by a week only if the Textile Council delayed the strike vote scheduled for that evening. Batty saw this as an attempt to disrupt the Textile Council at the last minute. He countered that it wasn't possible to postpone the vote, but the union leaders offered to delay counting the ballots. The Manufacturers' Association refused this compromise, and Ashley suggested that Batty delay the count anyway as a show of good will in order to press the mill owners to postpone the wage cut.

Samuel Ross, Abraham Binns and William Murdoch. Ross had been a union leader for 35 years when the strike started, but his influence was waning. His union, the mulespinners, had been replaced almost completely by ring spinners, who needed less skill to spin yarn. Binns was at the height of his power as a union leader. Trained in England as a weaver, Binns completely understood the complexities of modern weaving. Murdoch, a leader with the Textile Mill Committees, was well versed in labor organizing but new to the city and knew little about textile work.
Standard-Times

When the union leaders brought the sealed ballots to the Textile Council meeting that evening, two thousand textile workers packed the Bristol Arena. Rumors of a private meeting with Mayor Ashley earlier in the day offered hope for a quick settlement but probably also raised suspicions of a sellout among some in the audience. The *Evening Standard* had reported that James Simpson of the carders union had met privately with Ashley that afternoon against the advice of the other union chiefs. Abraham Binns called the mayor's office when Simpson was there, trying to dissuade him from meeting with Ashley. As a member of the Board of Commerce and the Welfare Board, Binns had the most political influence of any labor leader in New Bedford, but Simpson ignored Binns and continued his meeting with the mayor.

Another, deeper split was developing within the mill workers' ranks. Fred Beal from Lawrence and William Murdoch from Providence, militant labor organizers with a vision of an industrial union that would unite all textile workers, arrived in New Bedford a few days before the strike vote armed with ten thousand leaflets urging the textile workers to strike. Veterans of other New England strikes, they were trying to build the Textile Mill Committees (TMC), an organization that had originated in a Passaic, New Jersey, strike two years earlier. Beal and Murdoch warned the mill workers that delaying the count would allow the Textile Council leaders to count the ballots in secret and then announce that the vote had been against a strike. Many at the meeting supported the TMC's vision of one union in the industry, and most of the audience wanted the votes counted publicly.

The meeting opened quietly with Batty explaining the events of the past few days. The audience livened up when Simpson was called on to explain his meeting with Ashley. He admitted that nothing had resulted from the gambit, but he defended his right as a private citizen to meet with the mayor. Finally, the Textile Council began discussion of the strike vote. With the audience shouting, "Count the ballots," the Textile Council's leaders agreed to open the sealed ballots and tabulate the votes from each of the unions.

The result was 2,571 to 188 in favor of a strike on the following Monday, the day of the wage cut. Every union had voted overwhelmingly to strike.

No one doubted for a minute that the 2,571 union members who voted strike were speaking for the 27,000 workers employed in the mills at the time, and the greatest strike in the history of the city and perhaps the textile industry was imminent.

— John McKenna[11]

Despite this impressive show of support for a strike, Samuel Ross, the 1898 veteran and leader of the mulespinners union, complained that the public ballot count wasn't fair. Ross had told his members when they voted that the results would be withheld for one week, based on the Manufacturers' Association's offer to delay the wage cut. During the debate over when to count the ballots, Ross objected that few of his members were present, whereas many from the other unions were there. When he was overruled, Ross slammed the ballots on the table, told the other members of the Textile Council they could do as they pleased, and left the meeting.

HOW THE STRIKE WAS DECLARED			
	Total Vote	For Strike	Against Strike
Warp twisters	130	121	9
Weavers	1,140	1,105	35
Slasher tenders	110	93	17
Loomfixers	791	733	58
Carders	165	129	36
Mulespinners	254	232	22
Ring twisters	169	158	11
Totals	2,759	2,571	188

1928 Strike Vote.

Evening Standard

Textile Council leaders meet with Police Chief William T. Cole. Seated are William Batty, Squire Diamond, James Simpson, Chief Cole and Abraham Binns. Standing are Ernest Jones, Manuel Silva and Joseph Harrison. Chief Cole told Council leaders he would allow them to collect relief funds in the city but refused collection permits to the TMC.

Evening Standard

Ruffled feelings were smoothed out the next day as leaders from each of the unions issued public statements in support of the strike. But Ross still grumbled about the ballot counting, and Simpson accused Batty and Binns of an "unwarranted and vicious personal attack."[12] The Textile Council formed a general strike committee composed of the leaders of each of the unions, with Batty and Binns first among equals. When questioned about the Manufacturers' Association's offer of a week's postponement and Ashley's implied offer of mediation, Batty replied that 95 percent had voted in favor of a strike and that union members had been overwhelmingly opposed to delaying the count. Binns brushed off Ashley's offer, adding, "You can't mediate with starvation."[13]

Strike at a Glance

Mills On Strike

Corporation	# Mills	Looms	Employed
Acushnet	2	3,434	1600
Booth	2	1,338	600
Bristol	1	1,886	650
Butler	1	3,000	1,100
City Mfg. Co.	2	......	450
Gosnold	3	2,612	1,100
Grinnell	3	3,135	900
Hathaway	2	3,138	1,300
Holmes	1	......	800
Kilburn	2	......	1,200
Nashawena	2	6,100	2,700
Neild	1	1,640	574
N.B. Cotton	1	1,754	700
N.B. Spinning	2	300	200
Nonquitt Spinning	2	......	1,700
Old Colony Silk	1	......	200
Page	2	1,689	700
Pemaquid	1	450	325
Pierce Bros. Ltd.	2	1,200	390
Pierce Mfg.	3	3,426	1,000
Potomska	3	2,708	1,200
Quisset	1	......	600
Sharp	2	1,000	1,500
Soule	2	2,300	300
Taber	2	1,700	700
Wamsutta	8	3,247	2,000
Whitman	2	4,610	2,000
Totals	**56**	**50,667**	**26,989**

Mills Working

Corporation	# Mills	Looms	Employed
Beacon	2	......	1,250
Dartmouth	3	5,600	2,000
Firestone	1	......	1,000
Fisk	1	116	1,000
Goodyear	1	......	1,000
Gilt Edge Silk	1	260	115
National Spun Silk	3	......	2,000
Premier Silk	1	......	200
Totals	**13**	**5,976**	**8,565**

Solidarity was complete. The strikers completely shut down the mills that cut wages. The mills working were those that did not cut wages and therefore were not struck.

Evening Standard

Textile Council members gathered in front of the Labor Temple. Immediately following the strike vote, the unions received "hundreds of new members daily, and many former union members renewed their affiliations." The group, gathered in front of the Labor Temple, reflects the strikers' cheerful attitude in the early stages of the strike.

Ashley Scrapbook

On Sunday, the day before the planned strike, Ashley offered the Textile Council another postponement. The night before, he had met with the advisory committee of the Manufacturers' Association, which agreed once again to delay the pay cut by one week if the Textile Council would postpone the strike. The Council's executive board told Ashley that the offer was too late to present to the members, and that the board didn't have the authority to counteract the strike vote of the separate unions. In addition, the overwhelming support for the strike and the fear of appearing to bow to the mill owners' wishes made the union leaders wary of agreeing to a short postponement that probably would lead to a pay cut anyway. The mill owners consistently refused to meet with the union heads, and Ashley's plan offered no basis for negotiation between the Manufacturers' Association and the Textile Council.

The ten-cent wage cut imposed by the mill owners broke the camel's back — workers were real angry, and even though most of the workers were unorganized they poured out of the mills fighting mad. They were fed up with the wage cuts and the speedups, and it was almost as if everything was organized beforehand, but it wasn't. When the Textile Council rejected the ten percent cut and announced that they were gonna strike, all the unskilled people that they paid no attention to got out there. And they became the main force of the strike.

— Joe Figueiredo

Monday morning dawned sunny and cold. The Textile Council had done little to put its plan for a strike into action, and no one knew how effective the strike would be. Batty and Binns drove together from mill to mill to assess the situation. Delighted and somewhat surprised, they found crowds of mill workers at every gate, with hardly anyone going into work. Workers had set up informal pickets at many of the mill gates, but the general scene resembled a celebration more than a tense confrontation.

Some brought late breakfasts to the mills, and many wore their best clothes. At a time when they usually hurried into work, the mill workers chatted, laughed and sang songs.

There was some uncertainty about whether or not to go work. Some hoped they might find a sign, "No Cut," posted to cancel the strike. A few workers entered the mill to get personal belongings. Others were overheard to say, "If you'll go in, I'll go in too," but no one started in. Machines could be heard running near the doors where the crowd gathered. The noise gave the impression that some workers were in the mills, but with four or five cars in the parking lot, it was obvious the bosses were running the machines.
— Evening Standard[14]

Binns concluded, "It is a wonderful demonstration. I never saw such wholehearted support." At a mass meeting later in the day, Batty, who was celebrating his 38th birthday that day, added, "It is seldom given to any man to have such a widespread observance of his birthday."[15]

That afternoon, New Bedford's movie theaters reported record crowds for each showing. At the State Theater, five thousand people were turned away when the latest Lon Chaney movie, "The Big City," sold out in 15 minutes. Over three thousand mill workers also packed the Bristol Arena to listen to the union chiefs.[16]

The 1928 New Bedford textile strike had begun.

STRIKE IN 27 MILLS STARTS, HUNDREDS AT GATES ORDERLY

Binns States Walkout 100 Per Cent Effective—Batty Says Non-Union Workers Co-operate

MACHINES HEARD IN FEW PLANTS

Morning Shift Spinners Go in at Page— Throng Outside Sharp Indulges in Cheers and Snake Dance

New Bedford textile operates quietly went on strike at 27 mills this morning. After an early tour of the mill gates, labor leaders reported the walkout "100 per cent." Standard representatives who canvassed the situation found groups of voluntary pickets varying in number from a few to several thousands standing at the mill gates, all good-natured and orderly, and a few people going into the mills. Police reported no disturbances.
"It is a wonderful demonstration," declared Abraham Binns.

"Chiefs Assert Walkout Complete... A demonstration greeted Charles Rose, 518 Rivet Street, when he brought his loomfixers tools out of the mill this morning." Loomfixers had to cross the picket lines to retrieve their tools. The picketers celebrated Rose's return because even a few workers crossing the line would break their solidarity. Afterwards, Rose led a snake dance into the mill yard and out into the street again.
Ashley Scrapbook

"Perfectly peaceful, perfectly good-humored,
the New Bedford way of conducting a strike."

– Abraham Binns

"Outside the Nashawena, a shout went up and the crowd of workers streamed away after the gates were closed." [UPI / Bettmann]

CHAPTER 4

A NEW BEDFORD
KIND OF STRIKE

It didn't make very much difference whether there was a strike or not, my father was in and out. He'd come home in time to eat and then he was long gone. There weren't enough hours in the day. And when he was home, the phone was tucked under his chin. We just saw him coming and going. He had a way of coming home at noontime. He'd have a fast lunch, hop on the couch for 20 minutes, and tell my mother to wake him up in 20 minutes. He could recharge his battery in 20 minutes. And he was gone again. He was a busy, busy man.

— Harry Batty

The beginning of the strike was like a holiday for the workers, who had worked every day except Sundays in the hot and steamy mills since they were 12 or 13 years old. The Textile Council and its member craft unions expected a quick settlement. After the mill owners closed their gates on the second day of the strike, the Textile Council paid little attention to picketing. William Batty and Abraham Binns, as secretary and treasurer of strike relief funds for the Council, were content to make the rounds of the mills every day to make sure that the gates were closed.

The Textile Council held rallies for all textile workers once a week, where union leaders encouraged the thousands in attendance to keep up the fight. Notices were printed on the front pages of the city's newspapers, and the press carefully reported on discussions at the meetings. Batty was especially eloquent, contrasting the mill owners' tyranny with the democratic political system. He entertained the crowd by playing his cornet and led the singing of strike songs which he composed himself.[1]

PREVENT HUNGER IN NEW BEDFORD

This is an appeal for funds, but it is not an appeal to aid suffering of the people of some distant, heathen land. Dread poverty threatens thousands of New Bedford textile workers whose employment, and source of livelihood, has been eliminated by the shut-down of the local textile manufacturing plants of twenty-seven corporations. It is a self-evident fact that a continuation of this lack of means of earning a living will reduce New Bedford textile workers to a state of absolute destitution. And it is no answer to say that this condition is of their own making. Rightly or wrongly it is a fact that these textile workers believe they are fighting to obtain an existence wage for themselves and their families. Civilization recognizes that self-preservation is the first law of nature.

A group of prominent and responsible citizens prompted by the purest of humanitarian motives, have generously consented to serve as a Relief Committee to receive funds and distribute such funds impartially among the needy textile workers of this city. This Committee has decided that the elimination of hunger among these people shall have first call upon its funds. Help this Committee to prevent a spread of the dread disease of poverty and hunger.

Since the need is so great, you are urged to be as generous as possible in your donations, which alone will keep the hunger wolf from the doors of the homes of New Bedford textile workers, and to repeat your donations as frequently as possible to prevent the ascendency of dire poverty in your own city.

You should mail your donations to the New Bedford Textile Council Strike Relief Fund, P. O. Box No. 57, New Bedford Post Office, or to the Treasurer, New Bedford Relief Committee, Bates & Kirby Building, Pleasant Street, New Bedford.

Newspaper ad for strike relief. The Relief Committee was established late in April to collect funds. Volunteers were sent to mills, union halls, sporting events and working-class neighborhoods in New Bedford from as far away as Chicago.
Ashley Scrapbook

STRIKE RELIEF

Because starvation often had forced low-paid mill workers back to their jobs before, the first concern of the Textile Council leaders was relief. The craft unions could pay their seven thousand members about 20 percent of their usual weekly pay from their treasuries, enough to keep them out of the mills.[2] But the unions couldn't sustain these payments for long. In order to keep the mills closed, the Council had to raise money for the 20,000 mill workers who weren't union members. Most of these workers lived close to poverty when they were working; without their wages they soon would be destitute.

The Textile Council sought funds from other sources. Some union members who worked for the tire companies and other New Bedford mills that didn't cut wages pledged ten percent of their weekly pay to the strike fund.[3] Council members collected donations at sporting events, and their representatives collected money for strike relief in other New England cities. Other textile unions in New England, especially those in Fall River, sent contributions to the New Bedford strikers, who were alone in contesting the general wage cut.

There were no union funds to support a strike. There wasn't sufficient leadership amongst the craft unions to handle the job of raising money to support all of the 30,000 striking workers. So, in some of the union meetings, they asked for input from nonunion members as to how they could sustain the strike. They recruited a cadre of people who had some ability to go out and raise funds whether they belonged to the union or not. In time they would refer to them as walking delegates. And they hired my father.

It was my father's job to travel at union expense. They would supply him with transportation and enough for expenses. Not enough to support a fam-

Quartet of mill operatives prepares to leave for a Maine tour giving benefit performances to support the general strike fund. Left to right are Arthur Poineau, captain, juggler and balancer; Alyre Burgess, boxer; Wilfred Pontbriand, pianist and singer; and Pete Obut, general assistant. The troupe received Police Chief William Cole's well wishes before leaving. "He gave us a talk that meant something," said Mr. Poineau. "And I want to say he is one fine man."
Ashley Scrapbook

ily, but enough to support himself. They set him on the road and gave him a territory to cover — just like a salesman. Because the craft unions belonged to the AFL, they had a list of all of the big unions throughout the country. My father went to Philadelphia, New York, Baltimore, and all the way out to Detroit, St. Louis and Chicago. He had a full circuit. He was out there for five of the six months of the strike. His job was to determine when these unions were having their meetings, find out who the president was, and get permission from him to have ten minutes speaking time on the floor. Then my father would explain the plight of the New Bedford textile workers and plead for money for the New Bedford Textile Council, which represented all the craft unions in this area.

They raised thousands of dollars from these walking delegates. That's how they supported the strike for six months — with money from other unions around the country.

— Alfred Severs

The craft unions distributed strike funds directly to their members and organized a Citizens Strike Relief Committee to distribute relief to mill workers who were not members. The Committee was composed of clergy, owners of small businesses, and local professional people interested in "the cause of humanity and the desire to do civic duty as good citizens."[4] The Committee looked to the middle classes for funds, promising independence from the Textile Council and impartiality in the battle between mill owners and workers, but it received most of its funds from the Council's collections. The Committee gave out the money as vouchers for groceries from local storekeepers.

The 1928 Strike. A poem by Thomas Spellman, member of the Weavers' Union.

Men and women of New Bedford
Stick together in this fight.
Let the motto on your banner
Be for justice and for right

In the industrial depression
You did take a noble part
And ungrumbling shared the leanness
Of the floundering textile mart

By your courage and your patience
Toiling in the uphill rut
You've deserved a commendation
Not the stinging lash – the cut

You're not fighting for vain glory
A decent living is at stake
Knowing when you raise the standard
It is for your children's sake

Now the cheering news has reached us
That we'll get a helping hand
Of our noble fellow-workers
From all over our fair land

And our leaders, men of wisdom
Tell us that our cause is just
And that if we stick together
We will win, and win we must

Bread given out at Washington Club. Two weeks into the strike, private relief agencies were up and running. Made up mostly of striking workers, the Washington Club's soup kitchen was "their first response to the realization that the children of the striking families were certain to suffer." At a cost of $200 a week, open three times a week, the club fed approximately 1,200 children.
Ashley Scrapbook: *Times*

Most relief for nonunion strikers came from the city's public and private agencies, however. During the strike's second week, Batty, Binns and Textile Council President Joseph Harrison met with the city's Board of Public Welfare. They convinced the board that because the mill owners had closed the mill gates, nonunion workers couldn't work and therefore were eligible for public relief.[5] In order to focus city welfare payments on the nonunion strikers,

"A Real Act of Charity in the North End." George Darwish Harisee of Ganem & Co., a grocer at 298 North Front Street, poses with friends and neighbors who helped prepare more than 100 gallons of hot spaghetti soup. Harisee "proved to the mill operatives in the neighborhood that he appreciates their trade in the good times, and isn't forgetting them now."
Ashley Scrapbook: *Times*

the Textile Council leaders gave the Board a list of union members so they could be excluded from receiving welfare.

Applicants had to demonstrate they were destitute, without property, cars or money. This was true for most strikers, and thousands flooded the office. The Welfare Board gave out about $10,000 per week to the strikers, several times as much as the Citizens Relief Committee did.[6] Private organizations, such as New Bedford Family Welfare, the Catholic Welfare Bureau and the Soldiers and Sailors Relief, also gave small amounts of aid to striking workers not receiving strike pay from the craft unions.[7]

The strikers received help from the property owners and merchants in their neighborhoods. Sam Collins, the local boxing promoter who owned the Bristol Arena, refused to charge the Textile Council rent for its meetings.[8] "It was for a good cause and I could not see myself taking the money which could be used to better advantage by the textile operatives."[9] Collins later donated a railroad carload of potatoes to the Council.[10] Grocery stores extended credit to strikers, pharmacies and other small shops cut prices, barbers offered free haircuts and landlords reduced rents, in some cases cutting them in half.[11] But most mill workers stopped paying rent and many moved during the strike to avoid rent collection,

"Pails Prove Best For Carrying Soup." Children with empty milk bottles, pans and pails line up for their portions of soup and bread at the Washington Club. All 1,200 were fed on this day. Served from 75-gallon kettles, "it was none of your thin, watery charity soup, either. It was good, rich, thick pea soup, with bits of well-cooked meat floating in it and plenty of barley sinking to the bottom of the pail to be spooned up last." At right is a line of children at the Workingmen's Club in the North End.
Ashley Scrapbook: *Times*

"Bread Line at the Store of Henry Coury." At this *"dry and fancy goods store at 87 Collette Street, 500 loaves of bread were given out to strikers this noon."*
Ashley Scrapbook: Times

some moving in with relatives and other families.[12] Landlords, many of whom were mill workers themselves, felt the pinch especially towards the end of the strike in the fall, when city tax payments came due. Landlords tried to reduce rents further in hope of collecting something, but most collected little or nothing during the strike.[13]

I remember also how hard people worked to get by without having much. They had some strike benefits, but those petered out after a while. I can remember in my home at that time, there were six of us. We'd go to the store for a soup bone, and they'd boil the dickens out of it, although the kids that I went to school with figured that my father was still getting his wages. My father said if they were not getting wages, he wouldn't take them even though he was working as hard, probably harder than when things were good.

— Harry Batty

Support for the strikers came also from their own organizations. The Washington Club, a workingmen's club founded by the English textile workers in 1892, quickly opened a soup kitchen where children received soup, bread and lollipops. The club first worked for three days a week but began to operate daily when the crowd of children grew from 800 to 1,500. The club was in the South End near both the English and Portuguese neighborhoods, and the mostly English club members took pride that they didn't

Soup lines at the Washington Club. "Children, large and small, tiny ones clutching the hands of big brother or big sister, dark eyed Portuguese children with tangled black curls, tow-headed Saxon-faced children, children in neat boots and good coats, children in ragged hand-me-downs and out at the toes, fat red cheeked children who looked as though they had never lacked a square meal in their lives, and thin pale children who needed the generosity of the Washington Club if ever a child did... 'As long as there is a dollar in the treasury, it will be expended this way,' said Club President Fred Duckett."
Ashley Scrapbook: *Times*

The Washington Club, 1916. President Fred Duckett said, "It is the largest organization of its kind in the world. Its membership is entirely made up of workingmen, English born or of English parents, and Protestant." In 1992, the Club celebrated its 100th anniversary.
Standard-Times: Times

discriminate against Portuguese children. Because almost all members of the club were striking textile workers, the treasury soon ran out, but the soup kitchen continued on donations from city grocers and merchants.[14] By the end of the strike the club was feeding two thousand to three thousand children per day, and Fred Duckett, the club's president, estimated that it had given out 250,000 loaves of bread during the strike.[15] Smaller soup kitchens operated in the North End at the Workingmen's Club and at the Canadian Club.

Everybody had a sense of commitment. Store owners let people run up tremendous bills. Landlords cut rents until they barely met their tax and water bills. There was support for the worker because the worker was just about getting along, treading water, and no one could see how he could make ends meet with a 10 percent cut. People felt that the strikers were justified in what they were doing.

— Beatrice Pacheco

Bread line at the Washington Club. "Every Tuesday, Thursday and Saturday the above scene with two thousand to three thousand children has been the rule during the strike. The Club gives out 2,000 to 2,500 loaves of bread and 250 gallons of soup to the children on these days. The line extends from the club house on South First Street to Brock Avenue each day."
Ashley Scrapbook: Evening Standard

During the second week of the strike Thomas McMahon, president of the AFL-affiliated UTW, arrived in the city. He looked to recruit New Bedford's textile unions, which had participated in the founding of the UTW in 1901 but had left the national organization more than ten years before the strike in a dispute over jurisdiction and dues. Because UTW membership had dropped sharply from its peak in 1920, McMahon needed new members. He tempted the Textile Council's leaders with access to the AFL's greater resources and membership without dues during the strike. But Council leaders, worried as always over local autonomy, drove a hard bargain. They agreed to join the UTW only if each of their craft unions kept its own treasury and property, and the Textile Council joined the UTW as an autonomous unit, subject only to consultation with the national organization.[16]

SUPPORT FOR THE TEXTILE COUNCIL

The Council needed allies to pressure the mill owners to withdraw the pay cut. The democratic ideals of fairness and justice still existed in the city's small-town atmosphere, and the mill owners were susceptible to moral as well as economic arguments.[17] The Council also called on the political support it had built over the years.

At the start of the strike, public officials, including Mayor Ashley, trod lightly in the conflict, trying to walk a fine line between the mill owners and the Textile Council. Over the previous 30 years, the Textile Council had won its place in New Bedford political life. Samuel Ross, head of the mulespinners and the most successful politician among labor leaders, had served in the state legislature for 20 years and at the time of the strike was a member of the State Board of Arbitration and Conciliation, which either party in a labor dispute could call in to mediate conflict.

Each of the city's three newspapers, the *Evening Standard*, the *Morning Mercury* and the *Times*, opposed the wage cut, objecting to the workers' low

225 GALLONS OF SOUP CONSUMED

2,200 Loaves of Bread and 2,000 Lollipops Distributed to Children

Washington Club's Line of More Than 2,000 Longest Since Strike Began

More than 2,000 youngsters were fed with 225 gallons of soup, 2,200 loaves of break and 2,000 lollilops by the Washington club Saturday noon.

Mayor Ashley feeding pigeons outside City Hall. Good-natured and well-liked in the community, his loyalties were put to the test during the strike. An editorial comment in the Boston News Bureau, *July 28, expressed a widely held view: "Seeking to please all parties, he has succeeded in satisfying none."*

The Laggard. The Evening Standard *exhorted mill owners to "adopt business-like, modern methods of styling, trademarking, merchandising, and advertising of their wares to gain and hold markets."*

Standard-Times: Ashley Scrapbook

wages and the detrimental effect the wage cut would have on local business. The press aided relief efforts by praising contributors to the Citizens Relief Committee, usually on the front page. The newspapers also questioned the mills' finances and criticized the mill owners' greed and their outdated methods of management, advertising and sales. Editorials called for state intervention, asked why mill managers' salaries were not included in the cut and called on the mill owners to justify the wage cut.

Unlike the mill owners, who never were available to the media at the start of the strike, Batty and the other Textile Council leaders gave daily interviews and had exceptionally good relations with the press. Reporters usually were invited to meetings, and when strategy required privacy, Batty would give carefully prepared speeches to reporters and openly answer their questions. He seemed very comfortable with the press, which usually quoted him at his best.

The Textile Council also published a 12-part series by nationally renowned labor economist Dr. Norman Ware in the newspapers, showing that the wage cut was both unnecessary and unfair. Dr. Ware argued that the wage cut was unnecessary because New Bedford's major product, finely woven cloth, was not in competition with low-wage mills in the South and other areas that produced coarse cloth. He stated that wage cuts were unfair because profits were rising, not falling.

Newspaper articles by Frank Manning and Donald Thompson, who came from the Boston branch of the Young People's Socialist League to work for the Textile Council, spurred stockholders to enter the struggle. In

Rev. Donald Thompson, UTW President Thomas McMahon and Frank Manning. "There was a huge meeting of a couple of thousand workers in New Bedford and the speaker didn't show up. Mr. Binns of the weavers union came over to me and said 'Can you speak?' I said, 'Deliver a speech? I don't know, but I could try.' 'Well,' he says, 'I'm going to introduce you. We've got to have somebody.' So I made a speech which I think in retrospect was a little flowery but very sincere, and I guess the sight of a little black haired fellow in his twenties must have moved the audience because they gave me an ovation."
Ashley Scrapbook: Manning

a carefully written and widely published article, Manning argued that the mill owners in the Manufacturers' Association were not acting in the other stockholders' interests. He claimed that the mill owners' decision to cut wages was the latest in their history of bad management, following decades of paying themselves large salaries, placing their sons and other relatives in well-paying jobs, and ignoring modern business practices. Manning suggested that the smaller shareholders pressure the mill owners for a full disclosure of the mills' financial conditions.

WILL NEW BEDFORD MILLS TRAVEL ALONG THE ROAD TO PROSPERITY WITH THE OTHER INDUSTRIES?

W.S. EDGE

Prosperity via advertising. *Local newspapers repeatedly advised the mill owners to advertise. Here they're asked to join the automobile, soap and other toiletries on the road to prosperity. An unnamed mill owner answered, "What's the need of a cotton mill advertising? Everyone who buys from us knows exactly what we sell. It would be a pure waste of money."*
Ashley Scrapbook: Times

The seed fell on fertile ground. During the strike's third month, some shareholders actively opposed a plan for a few directors to sell and refinance the Whitman Mill. An overflow crowd of shareholders attended the meeting called to confirm the reorganization, and the crowded meeting had to be moved to the public library. Mary Leary, who led the stockholders' opposition to the sale, argued, "First the operators take a cut. It looks to me now like a wage cut for the minority stockholders."[18] Dr. Jacob Genensky, who had been refused access to the company's books when he visited the mill with an accountant and a deputy sheriff, called for a public accounting of the mill's financing. Leary and Genensky won the day, and management was forced to back down.

Newspapers and magazines outside New Bedford covered the strike. The *New Republic* and The *Nation*, national liberal weekly news magazines, charged that the New Bedford mill owners, who produced fine cloth, were using the wage cuts in coarse cloth to line their pockets, because they faced no competition from the South and were protected from foreign competition by stiff tariffs. The *New Republic* also reported that the low wages in New Bedford contrasted with the high cost of living. The magazine quoted a 1923 study of living conditions in New Bedford: "In few cities of the United States do the necessaries of life cost so much as in New Bedford."[19]

Surprisingly, trade newspapers for the textile industry blamed New Bedford management for its own problems. The *American Cotton and Wool Reporter*, the leading cotton textile weekly, wrote that the New Bedford mills were using selling methods of 50 years ago.[20] M. D. C. Crawford, the editor of Fairchild Publications, a leading publisher of textile magazines, also blamed archaic selling methods for the crisis and wrote that the wage cut could not stimulate demand and that mill owners should not punish workers for their own economic mistakes.[21]

The Spindle Slave. *Harvey O'Connor, a veteran labor reporter, started the* Federated Press, *a daily news service for labor issues.*
O'Connor

SPEEDING UP *the* SPINDLE SLAVE

by HARVEY O'CONNOR

Although national coverage never approached the yellow journalism of the 1898 strike, occasional articles tried to characterize the strike as a violent confrontation between destitute workers and greedy owners. The local newspapers perceived these reports as attacks on their city and took pride in the businesslike behavior of the Textile Council. The editor of the *Evening Standard* poked gentle fun at attempts to sensationalize the strike: "The writers who are satisfied with nothing short of clubs and bullets and bloodshed must have found New Bedford distinctly disappointing."[22]

The city's clergy also generally supported the Textile Council's demand for a return to the former wage level, and some openly supported the strikers. New Bedford had long been a center for activist clergy, who had been strong abolitionists and had formed an important link in the underground railroad before the Civil War. The Quakers who had dominated the city during the whaling days had fractured into several denominations, but most followed the Quakers' liberal, activist tradition. Most of the city's newer Protestant churches looked to the mills for parishioners, and some had been founded by mill workers, often with former workingmen as ministers.[23]

Many Protestant ministers worked behind the scenes to stop the pay cut before the strike started. When this failed, most preached on Sunday, the day before the strike was scheduled to start, about economic justice and a fair wage.[24] Although most were careful to state they weren't taking sides in the conflict, their sermons strongly opposed lower wages. Rev. Albert Vachon of the Immanuel Baptist Church said, "It is a black, hellish crime to make people work for less." Rev. Henry Williams of the First Baptist Church compared the strike to Moses's leading the Israelites out of Egypt. Others, such as Rev. Linden White of St. Martin's Episcopal Church, were more careful in their remarks, calling for a conference between the mill owners and the leaders of the Textile Council. Few if any of members of the clergy looked on the strike as the unions' fault.

EXPERT DECLARES WAGE CUT CANNOT STIMULATE DEMAND

M. D. C. Crawford Says Mills Should Not Punish Workers for Own Economic Mistakes

BLAMES ARCHAIC SELLING METHODS FOR CRISIS TODAY

Regrets New Bedford Must Learn Lesson So Painfully

EDITOR'S NOTE—The Times believes that this statement on the New Bedford wage cut and the general failure of the New Bedford mills to take effective action to stimulate such a demand for their goods that a wage cut need never have been considered is one of the outstanding contributions yet made by a disinterested but thoroughly well-posted outsider towards a settlement of the present crisis here.

'CONSIDER MILL WAGES FIRST, PROFITS LATER,' PLEAD PASTORS

Three Churchmen Assert Present Industrial System Is Obsolete, Inadequate, Contrary to Christianity — Call Upon Leaders and Workers to Accept Revision

An appeal for a revision of industrial relations, to apply [...]ood [...]ord

COMMERCE BOARD OFFICIAL ASKS THAT MILL MANAGERS TAKE CUT

City Employes Also Should Voluntarily Reduce Wages 10 Per Cent, Says Frank J. Leary, in Order to Clear Up Labor Situation Here—"Future at Stake"

Clearing of the labor controversy which befogs the industrial situation here would be facilitated by a voluntary 10 per cent reduction in wages of mill executives, city government and School

Civic opposition. Newspapers, the clergy and owners of small businesses strongly opposed the wage cut and sided with the Textile Council.

Ashley Scrapbook

The clergy continued these themes in sermons during the strike's early weeks and in the third week began meeting to discuss plans to end the strike. Clergy members tended to meet with others of their denomination, preparing for general discussions in the Ministerial Union and the Council of Churches.

In the fourth week of the strike, three Methodist pastors sponsored an appeal to the mill owners to put wages before profits.[25] The Methodists could not convince other clergy to sign their appeal, but later in the strike an organization of Unitarian ministers and an Episcopal bishop issued public statements in support of the strikers.

The clergy also participated in relief. Of the 14 officers and board members of the Citizens Relief Committee, ten were members of the clergy, with Reverend Hugh Gallagher of St. James Catholic Church as treasurer.[26] Father Gallagher, the head of the Catholic Welfare Bureau, also collected money for the soup kitchen at the Washington Club and took charge of relief operations in the South End neighborhood where most Textile Council members lived.

Respected community leaders who supported the Textile Council against the wage cut. Rev. Linden White, pastor of St. Martin's Church, Thomas Payne, president of the South End Businessmen's Association, and Father Hugh Gallagher, pastor of St. James Church. Rev. White reported to the newspapers that a private detective tried to bribe him to support the mill owners.

Standard-Times

At various times during the strike, civic organizations tried to bring together the mill owners and the Textile Council. Church groups and business organizations offered suggestions in the newspapers and met with Mayor Ashley. At the beginning of the strike, small business organizations in both the North and South ends of the city tried to mediate the conflict. Thomas Payne, president of the South End Merchants' Association, suggested on the *Standard's* front page that the Textile Council and mill owners try the issue before a jury.[27] As in a trial, both sides would be bound by the verdict after they had determined the rules of the debate and selected a jury. Neither side replied to his suggestion.

Efforts by business groups to end the conflict continued throughout the strike. At the end of May, two months into the strike, these groups merged into the Citizens' Mediation Committee, composed of five businessmen and three clergymen including Father Gallagher. In October, after several attempts to bring the Council and the Manufacturers' Association together, the Citizens' Mediation Committee offered the compromise that both accepted to end the strike. Batty admitted after the strike that the Council had operated behind the scenes to form these groups and encourage their participation.[28]

DIVISION AMONG THE MILL OWNERS

In contrast to the unity of the mill workers in closing the mills and enlisting support from the city's civic, business and religious leaders, the mill owners seemed disunited. The old guard, mill owners in their sixties from families who had held economic power in the city for generations, controlled the Manufacturers' Association. But the newest and largest mills, which produced cotton cord for automobile tires, were owned by outside interests and were not tied to the old guard. They were more interested in higher rates of production than in a wage cut. When the wage cut was announced, these companies offered their workers the old wage in exchange for higher rates of production.

Mill owners William Butler, Edward T. Pierce and Oliver Prescott. One of the most powerful men in the country, Butler managed Calvin Coolidge's successful campaign for U.S. President in 1924. He was chairman of the Republican National Committee and U.S. Senator at the time of the strike. Pierce succeeded his father, Andrew G. Pierce, as treasurer of the Wamsutta Mills. Prescott, a New Bedford lawyer like his father, was the first president of the New Bedford Board of Commerce.
Standard-Times

The Dartmouth Mill, which employed 1,500 workers producing the same product as the wage-cutting mills, also refused to cut wages. This deeply embarrassed the Manufacturers' Association, because the Dartmouth Mill, which wasn't a member of the Association, was the most profitable mill in the city and one of the most profitable companies in the United States. The owners of the Beacon Mill, also not related to the old guard, withdrew from the Association at the start of the strike and refused to cut wages.[29]

The five silk mills in the city, which did not belong to the Manufacturers' Association either, split over the wage cut. Three of the silk mills didn't cut wages and continued to operate throughout the strike, but the New Bedford and Old Colony silk mills cut wages by 25 percent, causing an immediate strike by the Textile Council.[30] Unlike the members of the Manufacturers' Association, however, the owners of these two silk mills agreed to negotiate with the Textile Council while the workers remained on strike. Negotiations continued for five weeks, when the mill owners agreed to withdraw the wage cut in exchange for an increase in the number of looms per weaver and other cost-cutting concessions.[31]

The owners of the tire companies, the silk mills and the Beacon Mill kept their opposition to the Cotton Manufacturers' Association quiet, but Walter Langshaw, owner of the Dartmouth Mill, openly questioned the wisdom of the wage cut and ridiculed his fellow mill owners. Langshaw wasn't a member of the old guard. He was born in 1859 near Bolton, Lancashire, the world center of finely woven cotton, where his family had established a cotton mill in 1790. He came to the United States with his family when he was seven and began working in the Lawrence cotton mills when he was nine. He moved to New Bedford when he was 32 to become

Dartmouth Manufacturing Company, circa 1912. Walter Langshaw, the owner of the Dartmouth Mill, was the only cotton mill owner not a member of the Manufacturers' Association. "I am a stranger within the gates. The blacklist even extends to my family and those who are employed by me… In some respects I have been as lonesome as a salmon would be in a millpond surrounded by suckers and tadpoles."
Joseph Martin, N. B. Whaling Museum: Langshaw

Walter Langshaw, president of the Dartmouth Mill, 1928. Statement from the Beacon Mill. "The root of the problem," Langshaw stated, "is overproduction." Langshaw admired "the loyalty of the workers to their cause, their cooperation and solidarity," but he believed that Council leaders were wrong in opposing changes in hours and work rules.

The owners of the Beacon Mill refused to cut wages and withdrew from the Cotton Manufacturers' Association over the issue. The Association published their version which argued that the Beacon Mill had withdrawn from the Association only in return for their workers withdrawing from the craft unions.

Standard-Times: Evening Standard

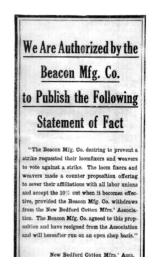

an overseer in the Potomska Mills and rose quickly to become a mill superintendent and then mill owner. Langshaw had been president of the Cotton Manufacturers' Association during the 1920 strike and lockout but had quit his position and withdrawn from the Association in one of several battles with the other mill owners.

Langshaw settled some scores with the old guard during the 1928 strike. In a long statement in the city's newspapers, Langshaw carefully showed that the mills, other manufacturing firms, banks and city service organizations were controlled by a "little group of old men" through a system of interlocking directorates.[32] He named names and made charges.

> *The responsibility for the trouble rests on those who are governed by the spirit of greed and intolerance, and who have little or no consideration to the effect of their arbitrary attitude… Our ills are mainly due to overproduction…due to expansion beyond requirements…. There are many who have been drawing salaries of from $10,000 to $25,000 a year as officials in the cotton manufacturing business whom I would pension rather than have in the employ of the Dartmouth Manufacturing Corporation.*
>
> —Walter Langshaw[33]

Langshaw was by no means a staunch union ally. Besides leading the mill owners against the Textile Council in 1920, Langshaw had battled the Council in 1926 in a strike over wages and weavers' fines. Rather than cutting wages in 1928, Langshaw used the issue to install the cost-cutting work rules that he had lost in the 1926 strike. The Council could not object to his speedup because he was an ally against the wage cut.

TROUBLE LOOMS AHEAD FOR THE TEXTILE COUNCIL

The strike was 100 percent effective in closing the mills. Although the city's newspapers, clergy and small business owners opposed the wage cut and the mill owners weren't united, economic conditions in the textile industry did not favor the strikers. After the strike started, prices of fine cotton cloth held constant, suggesting that buyers weren't worried about shortages during the strike. Industry analysts concluded that the strike had saved the owners from having to close the mills for the summer.

When almost no one crossed the picket lines on the first day of the strike, the mill owners closed their gates and began preparing for a long siege by taking down some of the machinery. They issued few statements to the press, but two days after the strike's start the Cotton Manufacturers' Association bought a full-page advertisement in each of the city's newspapers, arguing that other textile centers had cut wages and that it would be ruinous for them to pay more than a competitive wage.

Nevertheless, if Textile Council leaders maintained discipline within their ranks they could look forward to more favorable conditions for negotiations when market conditions changed. This strategy required that the unorganized workers, who formed a majority in the mills, follow the Council's leadership. But the lower-paid, mostly Portuguese, Cape Verdean and Polish workers had suffered long enough from their second-class status in the mills. This time they weren't willing to quietly follow the lead of the craft unions that long had excluded them.

This time they had a choice: the Textile Mill Committees came to New Bedford to challenge the Textile Council.

Mill workers' children sitting on a curb while their parents picket.
UPI / Bettmann

"On the Line, On the Line
On the Picket, Picket Line"

— Strike Song

Preparing for the July 4th parade held by the Textile Mill Committees. ⌈UPI / Bettmann⌉

CHAPTER 5

THE TEXTILE MILL COMMITTEES

There is no question in my mind that we put the backbone into the strike. There were leaflets against the pay cut, but it was pretty much a spontaneous affair. We put out leaflets, called meetings, and the workers responded. You didn't have to push anyone or hit anyone over the head. The people were very much incensed. They were living very close to the marginal line. We told the people that they were going to win or lose the strike because of what they done and not because of what we as leaders told them. We told them the strike would be won on the picket line, as a result we were able to build a great feeling and desire and need for attending the picket lines.

— Jack Rubenstein

The roots of the Textile Mill Committees (TMC) reached back to the founding of the Communist Party in the United States. In 1919, encouraged by the success of the Bolsheviks in Russia, a group split from the Socialist Party to form the Communist Party. The new organization joined the Communist International, a worldwide organization formed to unite the various national communist parties.

A struggle quickly developed within the International between two labor strategies: forming militant labor unions in opposition to the existing unions, or working from within the established unions to shift them towards more militant tactics and more revolutionary goals. V. I. Lenin, the leader of the Bolsheviks and the founder of the International, decided in favor of working from within the established unions.

For the U.S. communist labor leaders, this meant joining with the conservative AFL. Less than ten years earlier, in 1912, the UTW had fought the IWW in the Lawrence "Bread and Roses" strike. John Golden, president of the UTW, denounced the strike as a revolution. At a U.S. congressional hearing, Golden defended the clubbing and bayoneting of women and children by the police during the strike. During the following years, the UTW vigorously fought the various spin–offs from the IWW and other left-wing unions.

THE 1926 PASSAIC STRIKE

In 1926, Albert Weisbord, a young Harvard Law School graduate and Communist labor leader, welded together an impressive organization of women and men from several different mills spread throughout the Passaic region. In the deep snow of that winter, 16,000 strikers of many different nationalities closed the mills through mass picketing, paraded through the streets and held huge rallies. When the police turned water hoses on the strikers in the freezing cold, photographers sent pictures throughout the United States, and the strike became national news.[1]

Weisbord tried to bring the UTW into the strike several times, but the union refused to work with the Communists. When the mill owners offered to negotiate with the UTW if Weisbord left Passaic, he returned to New York amidst much fanfare, and the UTW took over. However, the mill owners wouldn't negotiate with the UTW any more than they would

Pickets at the White House during the 1926 Passaic strike. The United Front committees, the forerunner of the TMC, made the Passaic strike national news. They produced a seven-reel documentary movie, which was shown around the country to raise strike relief funds. The film is available from the Museum of Modern Art, New York.
UPI: Asher

with the Communists.[2] After six more months on strike, the UTW declared victory on the basis of a vague promise of union recognition from mill owners. Exhausted and penniless from being on strike for over a year, most workers probably were happy to return to work, but many were dubious about the UTW's victory. Their doubts proved correct. Within a few months, the mill owners had fired many strike leaders and continued their speedups and wage cuts.

As the Communist leaders watched the UTW abandon the strike, spending most of its efforts to discredit Weisbord and the Party, they realized that their strategy of working within the UTW couldn't succeed. In February 1928, the International reversed its earlier decision and directed its members to form unions to rival the AFL, focusing on the lower-paid, mostly immigrant workers that the AFL long had ignored.[3]

THE TMC TAKES CHARGE IN NEW BEDFORD

Fred Beal and William Murdoch, veteran labor organizers, were on the train to Manchester, New Hampshire, when they read that the New Bedford mill owners planned to cut wages. Selected by the Communist Party to organize textile workers in New England, Beal turned to Murdoch and said, "Murdoch, we shouldn't go to Manchester. Our place is in New Bedford.

TMC leaders Albert Weisbord, William Murdoch and Fred Beal. When they came to New Bedford Murdoch said, "Ours is a national body. We are fighting not only the cause of New Bedford's workers, but for textile operatives throughout the country... As the New Bedford wage controversy goes, so very likely will go the textile situation countrywide."

Standard-Times, Ashley Scrapbook

Let's go there and organize a strike."[4] Murdoch agreed. They got off the train at the next stop and returned to Boston, where they convinced the district party leader that New Bedford was more important than Manchester. After working all night printing leaflets urging workers to strike, they left for New Bedford and began passing them out at mill gates the next morning.[5]

Beal and Murdoch had travelled similar roads in different countries to become labor organizers for the Communist Party. Beal had worked in the woolen mills of Lawrence, a down-in-his-luck Yankee amidst the sea of recent immigrants and joined those immigrants in the "Bread and Roses"

Confrontation in Lawrence, 1912. The "Bread and Roses" strike in Lawrence was a violent confrontation over a wage cut during the winter of 1912. The strike attracted national attention when the National Guard attacked a crowd of women and children at the railroad station. Helen Taft, wife of President Robert Taft, attended congressional hearings on wages, working conditions and life in Lawrence. The strikers won their demands when William Wood, the city's major mill owner was implicated in a dynamite attack.

UPI: Cahn

strike in 1912. After the war, he returned to the mills and the militant labor movement. Murdoch, born the tenth of 11 children in Inverness, Scotland, was apprenticed to a machinist before he enlisted in World War I. After the war he emigrated to Providence, where he worked in several mills and became increasingly involved in labor organizing.[6]

Their paths crossed in Boston in 1927 when both joined the international movement to stop the execution of Nicola Sacco and Bartolomeo Vanzetti, labor organizers accused of armed robbery and murder in Braintree. Beal and Murdoch were attracted by the Communist Party's worldwide connections and its ability to organize large groups of workers. For their part, party leaders wanted Beal and Murdoch to implement their new strategy of forming militant textile unions in opposition to the AFL unions.

Beal and Murdoch found a welcome reception in New Bedford from the 20,000 Portuguese, Polish and other immigrant mill workers who long had been excluded from the craft unions. A few Portuguese workers, some of whom had been union organizers in Portugal and others who had been members of the IWW, helped Beal and Murdoch distribute leaflets.[7] This connection gave the organizers entry to the Portuguese community.

I went to the first meeting three days after the strike started. My father said, "You're on strike, go to the meetings." I think he was sorry later, but that didn't matter.

— Eula Mendes

"Outsiders Who Enter Wage Fight Here." On the second day of the strike, Murdoch and Beal pose with their aides outside their local office. The same day they opened their office, William Batty walked in and told them, "You are no good to anybody. You do not help the workers, you divide them. You are professional agitators. And I tell you, Murdoch, if you try to start anything here there'll be trouble." "We will do what we came here to do, Batty," replied Murdoch.

Evening Standard

Young TMC organizers Eula Mendes, Joe Figueiredo and Jack Rubenstein, who said, "I was born in Brownsville, a section of Brooklyn. My father was a wood turner. Brownsville was very political. To give you an example, the Democrats and the Republicans made a coalition to defeat the Socialist candidate. Every Saturday night, there were five or six speakers on the streets, Socialists; they'd speak on anything."
Standard-Times: Rubenstein

I was going to school in Boston and I noticed an advertisement for Pinkerton Guards—anticipating labor trouble in New Bedford. So I came back home to tell my father. Some so–called radicals had already asked him to help organize the French workers. My father was a loomfixer, but he couldn't get a job because years ago he had organized for the Industrial Workers of the World, the IWW. So he had gone into the construction game because he couldn't get a job in the mills.

— Al Saulnier

On Monday, April 16, the first day of the strike, Murdoch and Beal were joined by several veterans of the Passaic strike. They set up headquarters in the South End and announced a mass meeting for that Wednesday.

Fred Beidenkapp, president of Workers International Relief (WIR), addresses large crowd at Cove Street dump — the Kilburn Mill is in the background. The WIR was a relief organization run by the Communist party.
UPI / Bettmann

Although Batty and Binns bitterly denounced the group and warned workers to stay away from the meeting, over 500 mill workers attended. Even the most conservative New Bedford newspaper called the meeting a success.[8]

> *The people were dissatisfied with the craft unions. The unions were never too effective, not even the loomfixers except that they were probably successful in settling more grievances for their members. And we were pretty much welcomed. The craft unions practically held no meetings. We had meetings all the time and even the Textile Council people were coming to our meetings. Later on they were holding meetings too, once or twice a week. We were holding them every other day or so.*
>
> — Jack Rubenstein

"On the Line," 1928 strike song.

On the line, on the line
 On the picket, picket line
Boys and girls together
 In all kinds of weather
Singing on the picket, picket line

Picket line at the Acushnet Mill. Women, men and children walk the line; a nun can be seen with her umbrella.

UPI / Bettmann

The TMC quickly took the alienation and frustration of the unskilled, lower–paid workers, who had been excluded from the craft unions, and turned it into an enthusiasm unrivaled in previous New Bedford textile strikes. Daily picketing, meetings, rallies and soup kitchens created excitement, purpose and unity behind the strike in the Portuguese and Polish communities. Thousands walked the picket lines and attended rallies organized to educate and entertain. The TMC concentrated its efforts in the immigrant neighborhoods located around the mills in the North and South ends of the city and left the center of town, where the mill owners lived and commerce reigned, to the Textile Council. Organizers

went to people's homes to encourage participation. Families picketed as groups—women with babies in their arms, young children walking alongside.

The TMC's message did not end with opposing the ten percent wage cut. The group demanded a 20 percent wage increase, a 40-hour work week, equal pay for equal work, an end to the speedup, no discrimination against union members and an end to child labor.[9] Their plans called for a single union covering all textile workers in the city and a democratically elected executive committee.

> *We wanted a union that would take in all of the textile workers. We called for an industrial type of union instead of a craft union, and that was quite progressive at that time because most of the unions in the United States at that time were craft unions. The whole idea was to get all the textile workers in one mill to belong to one union and all of the textile workers to belong to a single textile union.*
>
> — Eula Mendes

These plans proved too ambitious, because the frantic pace of the strike didn't allow time for a complicated internal structure. Beal and Murdoch directed activities, while labor organizers from Passaic teamed with local grass roots leaders to direct strike activities. Jack Rubenstein, who had led the picket lines in Passaic, directed the TMC pickets against those mills that were rumored to be operating or that were selling cloth from their inventories. Because the TMC's goal was to unite workers from all mills into a single union, workers were told to picket the mills closest to their homes, whether they worked there or not.

Family pickets. *"This picture was taken at the Acushnet Mill this morning (May 8) as about 100 radicals marched their babies past the gates."*

Evening Standard

TMC picket line at the Hathaway Mill. *"Observers from the Textile Council were in evidence at every mill. They did not march but stood nearby in small groups chatting, and wherever a crowd of curiosity seekers gathered, the observers mingled with the crowd. Textile Council officials made their daily morning tours to keep in touch with the situation."*

Ashley Scrapbook

Children in the TMC picket line at the Hathaway Mill. "It is a crime to allow those children in the line," declared William Batty. "If trouble should start they would be trampled on the first thing and possibly killed. The whole thing is a publicity stunt, and they would all be better off in bed."
Ashley Scrapbook

Picket lines often would march from mill to mill before gathering for a mass meeting at TMC headquarters. After hearing local and sometimes national leaders, everyone would march to one of the mills and continue picketing. Hundreds and often thousands of mill workers and their families would spend the day on the picket lines and at TMC rallies. Many more people would troop to the mills to watch and shout encouragement.

As they had in Passaic, the TMC leaders included women and children in the strike activities. Ann Washington Craton, a New York labor organizer and writer, told TMC members, "Make the strike a family affair. Women are better at this sort of thing than the men. They are more courageous than men. They will do more and suffer more… You women who cannot leave your children at home, bring them with you. Let them understand what the strike means, so that when they have to go hungry, and when they have to go to school in ragged shoes, they will know why. Educate them to be good union men and women for they are the workers of the future."[10]

Young women on the picket line, and Elizabeth Donnelly with children. Donnelly answered Batty's criticism: "They are of and with the working class…These children are forced to work at an early age… They do not receive a proper education; they do not have proper food…They ought, therefore, to learn what the conditions are under which they will work when they become men and women, to be educated to carry on the work of improvement their parents are doing now."
Standard-Times: Ashley Scrapbook

Elizabeth Donnelly, who had dropped out of Boston University to work as a labor organizer, helped put this rhetoric into practice. She led children on the picket lines, and at TMC headquarters she taught them the meaning of the strike. When the number of children increased and Donnelly needed more space, she asked Mayor Ashley for permission to use the city's playgrounds. Ashley refused, saying, "No, you can not have any playground or anything else that I have any control over for your damnable work with children, as long as I am in the Mayor's chair."[11]

The newspapers sided with Ashley against the TMC, hinting that Donnelly's request to Ashley was a publicity stunt to make Ashley look uncaring towards children. They argued that Donnelly didn't really want to use the city's playgrounds and wouldn't know what to do if Ashley had said yes.[12] They contrasted the children being fed by the Textile Council members at the Washington Club with the children marching in the TMC picket lines. An *Evening Standard* editorial titled, "Children First," went further: "We recall nothing more shameful unless it is the tactics of an invading army which forces the children of the defenders to march ahead of it."[13]

Stung by the newspapers' rhetoric, Donnelly and the TMC changed tactics. Children no longer marched alone but joined their parents on picket lines for the remainder of the strike. Often the police took the names of the children on the lines to check for truancy from school. But Donnelly continued to organize children's clubs which were youth activity centers with a union bent. Young women in their teens especially were drawn to Donnelly and the TMC. Before the strike, their lives were spent at work or at home. But during the strike, for the first time in their lives, they were allowed out on their own.

Elizabeth Donnelly leading children on the picket lines.

When you're up, you're up,
  When you're down, you're down.
But when you think you'll break the strike
  You're upside down!
Ashley Scrapbook

Coupons sold in support of the New Bedford strikers for 25 cents each told the prospective buyer of strikers beaten and clubbed on the lines. "Three hundred special police have been imported from Boston with the intention of terrorizing the strikers and forcing them back into the mills". This coupon was confiscated from the clothing of Augusto Pinto upon his arrest for disturbing the peace.
Ashley Scrapbook

Because the TMC had no treasury and most members couldn't collect from the Textile Council or its relief organizations, strike relief became a major activity for the new union. When Police Chief William Cole would not allow the TMC to collect money in the city, Murdoch replied that he expected harassment from local police. "The opposition to us here is very strong. Permits might be issued and then revoked; so we shall not try it. We will obtain our funds from other cities."[14]

Chief Cole also notified police chiefs in other cities that the Textile Council collectors were the official representatives of New Bedford strikers, and he asked them to stop the TMC representatives from collecting for strike relief in their cities. The communist relief organization, the Workers' International Relief (WIR), promised large donations. However, like the UTW and the other AFL unions that promised much, it didn't deliver. Little money from the WIR actually reached the city.

The TMC established committees on picketing with picket captains. They also established a relief committee which tried to get food and financial support. A carload, sometimes two and three carloads of us, would go to Fall River and go to working-class neighborhoods. We knew the majority of the people living in these areas were textile workers. We would go to their homes. They had a little sticker on them which said, "Support and relief for the New Bedford strikers." We would also go to places like Brockton, Lawrence, Malden, Pawtucket and Providence.

— Joe Figueiredo

The city's relief agencies and private charities also chose the Textile Council over the TMC. Batty and Binns maintained close contact with city welfare officials, and strikers needed cards signed by the Textile Council to apply to the Citizens Relief Committee.[15] The police took photographs of people on the TMC picket lines and distributed them to the city agencies and the Citizens Relief Committee so they could stop TMC members from getting strike relief.[16] Later in the strike, when property and bank books were used to bail out arrested TMC picketers, the court gave city agencies the names of people supplying bail to show that they owned property and shouldn't collect strike relief.[17]

The Workers' International Relief office in Boston repeatedly shipped food supplies to New Bedford. At other times, members of the TMC would go to Boston stores by car and collect bread, canned goods and meats.

Ashley Scrapbook

The TMC relied mainly on the tightly knit Portuguese and Polish communities that always had provided for their own in need. Most families were used to poverty because they earned subsistence wages and had learned to do without. Although rent and other payments could be stopped with little effect, people still had to eat. Family gardens helped, and Portuguese dairy farmers, bakers and fishermen donated milk, bread, and fish, which were distributed from TMC headquarters on Scott Street.

We had a few trucks, and they'd go to Rhode Island to the little grocery stores and get the bones that they would throw out to make soup with. It was all filled with maggots…but they would come back and put that in the great big vats that they got. They would boil that and the scum would come on top. They would skim that. The rest of it was the broth that they used to make soup. Then they'd go out and pick up whatever they could get to make it, give it a body. And that's what you had to eat. You'd have to bring your own dish, and you could get one cup of soup, including the kids.

Someone knew how to bake bread. We had torn down Giusti's Bakery on Water Street to the south of the Orpheum, and we had two big ovens that were set up in a corner of our property. They had these big vats on wheels, made out of cypress, where they'd mix the dough. They used to work all night.

— Al Saulnier

TMC workers with donated food and milk on an empty lot on South Water Street. *By the end of August, 39,356 people were getting assistance at the various relief stations throughout New Bedford. Generous donations came increasingly from cities such as Providence, Boston, Fall River, Lynn and Pawtucket.*

UPI / Bettmann

The Textile Council Responds to the TMC

The Council leaders vigorously opposed the new union. The TMC's attraction for unorganized workers and even for some Textile Council members weakened the Council's control over the strike. Over the past 30 years, Batty, Binns, Ross and the other leaders successfully had used the unity of the skilled workers to confront mill owners when they could, and to accommodate them when they couldn't. They would not give up these gains easily to accept the TMC leaders and their mostly Portuguese and Polish followers, who threatened the Council's social, political and economic status as labor leaders in New Bedford.

At first the Textile Council leaders publicly ridiculed the TMC effort. Binns, expecting a small turnout for the TMC's first mass meeting, said, "We'll let the Textile Mill Committees conduct their own funeral."[18] At the same time, Council leaders joined the growing chorus in the city's newspapers in calling Beal, Murdoch and the other TMC leaders communist invaders and outside troublemakers leading a revolution in New Bedford. Batty was especially virulent toward the TMC organizers: "They lead the workers not to strike but to slaughter," he said in a prepared statement to the city's newspapers.[19]

The word "reds" was used a lot in the commercial press. They tried to take the focus away from the strike and what it was all about. They tried to

"Strawberry Shortcake," 1928 strike song.

Strawberry shortcake, huckleberry pie,
 Who gave the bosses a punch in the eye?
We did. We did. And who are we?
 We are the members of the TMC.

Outside the Neild Mill. *"Police keeping the strikers on the move, preventing gathering of large groups."*
UPI / Bettmann

portray it that we had an enemy here when the real enemy was the mill owners. They fabricated and exaggerated and invented. What happened, however, was it boomeranged as far as the mass of the textile workers were concerned. They were involved in the strike, and it didn't happen the way these newspapers presented it.

— Joe Figueiredo

STRIKE SETTLEMENT
MAY BE HASTENED BY
FEAR OF RED MENACE

Rapid Progress of Radical Movement
and Impossibility of Treating with
This Element Disturbs Labor Chiefs
and Mill Men

By A. A. TALMAGE

Although these strategies may have influenced the Council's members, they had little effect on Portuguese and Polish mill workers. Many didn't speak English, and those who did interpreted these attacks as evidence that the Textile Council and the city's elites were united against them. Also, some Portuguese workers, especially those from the Continent, knew the difference between a labor strike for higher wages and a political revolution to overthrow the government. They had witnessed the overthrow of the Portuguese king by the socialists in 1915 and the political shifts between left and right in Portugal afterwards. Shrill denunciations of communism and emotional appeals to American values didn't convince the Portuguese mill workers to leave the TMC. For them, the TMC was fighting for higher wages and equality with other workers, principles easily identified with American democracy.

Young women among defendants. Antone Reis, Mrs. Bernada T. Pina, Miss Marion Botelho, Mrs. Antonio Santos. "The most active people in he strike were the Portuguese, not only the people from the mainland, but also from the islands, from the Azores, from Cape Verde, from Madeira. The people from the islands were a little more conservative, but they joined in, and the strike was pretty solid among the Portuguese."

Ashley Scrapbook: Mendes

And people were not concerned because the way we approached them was, "They call us communist because we fight for you." We put it in such simple terms. We talked about the class war in terms of concrete illustrations that they could understand. We said the bosses and the newspapers—they're all against us—they make their money out of us. The more they give us, the less there is for them.

— Jack Rubenstein

When the TMC's picket lines began to build, the Council's leaders had to win back the leadership of the strike. The Council had stopped picketing after the mill owners closed their gates on the first day of the strike, but the TMC used mass picketing and daily rallies to build up its membership. While making his daily rounds of the mill gates, Batty came upon a large TMC picket line at the Wamsutta Mills and spotted Beal.

Fred Beal with bodyguard on the picket line and William Batty. The first time Batty saw Beal on the picket line, he walked up to him and punched him in the nose. Batty defended himself, saying, "I considered it the only way I could retaliate for Beal's written attack on me at Lawrence. I couldn't prosecute him; he's got nothing. It would do no good to argue with him. Physical force was the only means of satisfaction I could see." Beal responded, "I have nothing against him personally. As far as I am concerned the incident is closed."
Standard-Times: Times

He walked up to Beal and punched him in the face. A wild melee followed. TMC supporters attacked Batty and, according to Beal's statement in the newspapers, Beal and Murdoch tried to defend him. Batty told the newspapers, "I would have done the same to him if I had found Beal in New York, Boston, or anywhere else. In a story, he called me a traitor to the cause of labor… I warned Murdoch to tell Beal to keep out of my way or I'd punch his nose."[20] Batty probably suffered the most physical damage, a few bruises and a torn coat, but showed his members that he was an active and courageous leader.

I remember one time and I think my father had been in Patterson, New Jersey, when he met Beal who was causing trouble there. My father said to Beal, "Don't ever come to my hometown." Beal did come and when my father saw him, he got out of his car and walked through the crowd and took a swing at him.

— Isabelle Batty Milotte

In response to the TMC's daily actions, the Textile Council broadened its vision of strike activities. The Council held weekly open meetings in the Bristol Arena and rallies at Buttonwood Park in the city's center that thousands of mill workers and their families attended. National union leaders and well–known politicians addressed huge crowds, who quietly listened to long speeches. In contrast to the Council's practice, many of the speakers spoke openly in favor of socialism and the unity of all workers.

Norman Thomas, Socialist Party candidate for U.S. President, addressed three thousand listeners at a Council rally and donated over $500 to the strike fund.[21] A. J. Muste, founder of the Brookwood Labor College, a socialist–oriented school for training labor organizers, spoke several times. August Claessens, member of the Socialist Party, well–known humorist, and education director for the Rand School of Social Science, another school for labor organizers, held classes in public speaking.[22]

Norman Thomas and William Batty. Thomas was the Socialist candidate for U. S. President in 1928. Although he never was a factor in the national elections, Franklin Roosevelt and the Democrats adopted some of his ideas, such as social security, in the 1930s.

Ashley Scrapbook

Sadie Reisch, Rose Schneiderman, Josephine Kaczor. Reisch was an organizer for the Women's Trade Union League, Schneiderman was president of the organization, and Josephine Kaczor was a graduate of the Brookwood Labor College. The Coalition of Trade Union Women and Women in Leadership Development carry on their tradition today.
Standard-Times, Ashley Scrapbook

Women, who numbered about half of New Bedford's mill workers, long had been ignored by the Textile Council. Although about one–third of the Council members were women, all of the Council leaders were men.[23] The Council tried to counter the TMC's focus on women by bringing in women speakers, encouraging women to come to membership meetings, and holding special events for them. Rose Schneiderman, president of the Women's Trade Union League, and Esther Friedman, lecturer from the Rand School, addressed several thousand people at a Council meeting.[24] Schneiderman told her audience, "In the old days, women always would work more cheaply than men. And as long as they held themselves cheap, they were cheap. You women who do men's work have got to remember that and organize along with your husbands…Don't let them divide you. One big union in the textile industry is its only salvation."[25]

When the crowds grew too large for a single location, the Council held simultaneous meetings in Brooklawn and Hazelwood parks in the North and South ends of the city. Rallies, where local and national speakers spoke, regularly were held on Monday afternoons, continuing the Council's practice of Monday membership meetings. Occasional assemblies and picnics also were held on other afternoons and evenings. At festivals, several thousand mill workers listened to the speakers and the music, ate, chatted and sang, while children played, and young people courted.

"Typical Group at Mill Gates As Strike Opens." A group of women textile workers standing outside the Nashawena Mill.
Ashley Scrapbook

Textile Council picnic at Brooklawn Park. Batty told the press, "Seeing that we gave a picnic for the South End at Hazelwood, we felt that this was coming for the North End." Then came a shout, "There'll be a ball game on the diamond. The winner will be the Textile Council and the loser the Wamsutta Club."

Ashley Scrapbook: *Times*

Many speakers remained in New Bedford to provide the usually staid Textile Council with a group of versatile young labor organizers to carry out more militant tactics.[26] Frank Manning and Donald Thompson came from Boston at the start of the strike to work for the Textile Council and stayed until its end. Sadie Reisch, organizer for the Women's Trade Union League, and Josephine Kaczor, who had graduated from the Brookwood Labor College two weeks before she came to New Bedford, were sent by their organizations to aid the Council.

On a typical strike day, I would get up and picket one of the mills. I would then go to the office and see what I could do in the way of getting more enlists and more support—financial and otherwise. Then I would walk around to the bigger mills and pick out a different soup kitchen and stay to eat with the people. And very often I would have a speech to make before some particular group. All kinds of little things would occur. People would come to see me about some problems that they had, and very often at night, I would be invited to one of the strikers' homes for supper. No difficulty in understanding the language. They had good humor, some that I didn't always catch. They had their own songs and were always singing, "I want a pie with a plum in it," and so forth.

— Frank Manning

The soup kitchens for children, operated by Textile Council members, fed Council and TMC families alike. The Council also held weekly dances for young people at the Sharpshooters Hall, a French–Canadian

"Picket or Picnic at Sharp Mill Today. The Textile Council had 150 smiling pickets on duty at the Sharp when the gates opened this morning."

Times

"*Strikers Enjoy Card Games at North End...* There's no money on these tables because the strikers haven't any to put there. But they have a good time at the North End headquarters of the Textile Council." Many of the unions in the Textile Council owned halls where they held meetings and social events.

Ashley Scrapbook

club and opened recreation centers in the North and South ends of the city. Batty took pride in comparing the Council's activities for young people to those of the TMC: "That's the sort of thing to do in this strike. Feed the children instead of driving them into the picket lines. Give the young men and women wholesome recreation instead of dragging them out to mass meetings every five minutes to be taught the elements of communism... The other gang puts them out on the picket line; then they come here to get their breakfast."[27]

The Textile Council leaders also tried to attract the Portuguese, Cape Verdean, Polish and French–Canadian men and women, whom they long had excluded.

Manuel Silva, secretary–treasurer of the ring twisters union, which represented the lowest paid craft union workers, was given more prominence within the leadership of the Council. He spoke in Portuguese at mass meetings and asked Portuguese workers, whatever their jobs in the mills, to join his group or at least attend its meetings. But Silva never was successful in attracting Portuguese workers to the Council. At the special Council meetings for Portuguese workers, TMC members arrived in force to belittle the Council's recent conversion to solidarity.[28] When the TMC accused Father Manuel Salvador, pastor of St. John the Baptist, of advising workers to end the strike in his Sunday sermon, Father Salvador denied the charge and Silva was forced to side with the church and apparently against the strikers.[29]

The Council crossed the color line to invite African–American union leaders to speak at its rallies. Frank Crosswaith, organizer for the Pullman Porters Union, told a meeting in the Bristol Arena that attracted 900 listeners by the time he had finished speaking, "In the struggle between these two organized groups race and religion do not count. The manufacturers try to force you to recognize them. They pace French against Portuguese, Polish against English knowing that when they get them divided they can ride upon beds of ease for centuries to come as the employees remain divided."[30]

Horace Riviere, Andrew Izyk and Frank Crosswaith. Riviere was district organizer for the UTW. Izyk was a loomfixer, who became active in the TMC. Crosswaith, organizer for the Pullman Porters Union, told a Textile Council audience, "The Negroes bring to the labor movement their song, the only American music, their rustic humor and their loyalty. They are with you in this strike, as their's is your strike."
Ashley Scrapbook

To attract Polish members, the Council began a new union for all Polish workers regardless of their craft. However, the implications of seven craft unions and a Polish union weren't lost on most Polish mill workers. President Jan Kisiel of the Polish Textile Workers Union compounded the problem when he hinted that the strike could be settled with a cut of five percent instead of ten percent.[31] Most Polish strikers were in no mood to offer a wage cut, and the organization disappeared.

Special Council meetings for French-Canadian workers led by Horace Riviere, a veteran UTW organizer, proved more successful as hundreds of French-Canadian workers joined the Council's unions. Some became union leaders after the strike.[32] The TMC had much less success recruiting French-Canadian workers. In the middle of the strike, Felix Ouillette was named president of the TMC but soon resigned in a dispute over picket line tactics. He took most of his countrymen to the Textile Council with him, saying, "I don't believe there is another Franco–American in the TMC."[33]

But the TMC continued as the main force on the picket lines while the Textile Council preferred to avoid confrontation with the mill owners and the law. At the end of the strike's second month, after weeks of Batty's arguing that it already had closed the mills, the Textile Council resumed

"Josephine Kaczor from Salem Local 33 of the UTW, and Horace Riviere, UTW General Organizer led the Textile Council picket line at the Wamsutta Mill this morning." Josephine Kaczor was born in Salem and graduated from Brookwood College, an institute devoted to preparing labor leaders. "I consecrated myself to the labor movement," the 20-year-old Kaczor told the Times. *"Now I am here ready to do whatever the textile council directs. It is really the beginning of my career."*
Ashley Scrapbook

picketing.[34] The Council's picket lines were smaller than the TMC's, however, and usually the TMC maneuvered Council pickets into following their lines.

When a few and then hundreds of TMC pickets were arrested, the Textile Council claimed good citizenship for its members in contrast to the TMC's lawlessness. Finally, with the TMC leading the majority of mill workers and even attracting the Council's members, the Council's leaders had to yield the high ground and get down with the strikers. Led by Reisch, Kaczor, Manning, and Thompson, the Council defied court orders against picketing. Some members were arrested, and Batty, Binns and the other Council leaders spent a few hours in jail.

They didn't have the all-night picket lines the way we did. We had everything pretty well organized after a very short time. We had coffee and sandwiches ready for the pickets. We had lawyers ready in case they were arrested. We had bail bonds people, and we even had arranged if somebody got arrested who they would notify.

— Rev. Donald Thompson

By that time, the battle was being fought with a different enemy, however. No longer were the two unions the main antagonists in the strike. The mill owners awoke as if from a long sleep and began their assault.

TMC pickets under arrest. *When they ran out of patrol wagons, the police hired private trucks from New Bedford and other cities to carry prisoners. Here, TMC pickets are hauled to jail in a van owned by A.D. McMullen, Furniture and Piano Movers.*
UPI / Bettmann

Here the Battle is Bitter
The Fire is Hot

— Moshe Nadir

Captain Albert MacKinstry orders TMC leaders to stop parade. Jack Rubenstein and John Pelczor refuse. ⌈UPI / Bettmann⌉

CHAPTER 6

MILL OWNERS STRIKE BACK

The walls between the cells were about three- or four-feet thick stone, and no one was allowed to talk or say anything. When you filed out of your jail in the morning you had a wooden bucket that was put there during the night. You marched up to a big pit that had some chemicals in it, and the mixture of the chemicals and the night soil was the most revolting smell that I could ever remember in my life. And you marched by and emptied your bucket into the pit, and you marched back into your cell. Frankly, the two or three times that I was in jail, I didn't mind it a bit because I slept night and day, except that the mattress was kind of tough.

— Jack Rubenstein

The Textile Council long before had won its place in the city. The Council picketed the mills with little police interference and conducted meetings rent-free in public parks, community buildings and the Bristol Arena. New Bedford's ruling establishment treated the TMC very differently. TMC members were harassed by city officials, arrested by police and sentenced by the courts. When Mayor Ashley refused the TMC use of the city's parks and other public property, the union held rallies in vacant lots and city streets, always with an eye out for the police. Smaller meetings were held in empty buildings in workers' neighborhoods.

The city's newspapers also favored the Textile Council over the TMC. They carefully reported the Council's actions and treated Council leaders with respect, describing Batty, Binns and the others as cool, patient, law-abiding citizens and businesslike professionals. The local press portrayed the TMC leaders as invading strike agitators and romantic adventurers who were "tempestuous, excitable, unsteady, and even weak-chinned."[1]

As the strike wore on, the mill owners used their control over the legal, media, and civic institutions against both labor organizations and tried to end the strike on their own terms.

The Establishment vs. the TMC

At 6:30AM on May 8, police broke into TMC headquarters on Potomska Street. They evicted the 50 people preparing for picket duty, saying the building was not licensed as a meeting place and did not comply with fire and health regulations.[2] Deputy Police Chief Samuel McLeod, who led the raid, threatened to close the TMC's North End quarters in the Madeirense Sporting Club as well. Two weeks later, the Club banned the TMC from holding further meetings, declaring that it no longer supported the group and that the TMC hadn't paid its rent.

The TMC's space problems were solved when Oliva Saulnier, former mill worker and IWW member blacklisted from the 1912 strike, came to a TMC rally held in the city dump on Cove Street. After the rally, Saulnier offered the TMC free use of a property called Saulnier's lot, located near the mills in the South End. Saulnier's lot was an open space large enough to hold several thousand people, surrounded by buildings and fenced off from the street.

My father went over there and told the strikers, "I can't give you any money, but you can meet on my land." Our property was all fenced in. They put their own guards in there, and if you didn't have a card, you couldn't get onto the lot. You had to be a textile worker. Someone had to recognize you, or you had to have a pay envelope or a receipt of some kind to show that you had worked in a mill.

Fred Beidenkapp speaking at Saulnier's lot. Meetings were held daily at Saulnier's lot after the morning picket. The TMC headquarters was an ideal location. The lot was private property and was fenced off from the street, preventing the police from entering without just cause.
UPI / Bettmann

TMC speaker addresses the crowd at Saulnier's lot. *"The police never got in there. The New Bedford police didn't give us too much trouble. The only guy we had difficulty with was a fellow named McCarty. The newspaper guys were a bunch of bastards, too. They'd create a situation for a story. They had a deadline to make."*
UPI / Bettmann: Saulnier

We had a right to have meetings on our own property. We had a right to keep the police out as long as there was no disturbance, and the way to prevent a disturbance was to prove that everyone who came in had worked in a mill. They never had any trouble on our property. They met every day, about two or three hundred people, to decide what they were going to do that day, where they were going to picket and so forth. They had everything pretty well organized.

— Al Saulnier

I make my way through the northern streets to the Lot. Children are running about with swollen bellies, spindly legs and scabby ears.
"Where is the Lot, children?"
"The Lot?"
Their faces light up and for the moment they stop scrounging through the mountain of old iron scraps, to show where it is.
"My father is there."
"My mother too."
"And my three brothers."
"When I grow up, I will go out on strike. Give a penny Mister."

— Moshe Nadir

Ramboia: An Azorean folk song sung on the picket lines.

A ramboia, a ramboia
   Anda sempre a ramboiar.
Quem casar com a papo-seco
   Não precisa de trambalhar.

A menina do papo-seco, o ai!
   Não precisa de trambalhar, o ai!
A menina do papo-seco, o ai!
   Nunca precisa de trambalhar.

A ramboia, a ramboia
   Anda sempre a ramboiar.
Quem casar com a papo-seco
   Não precisa de trambalhar.

A woman who loves to dance
   Is always dreaming.
Whoever marries a dandy
   Does not need to work.

The dandy's girl friend
   Does not need to work.
The dandy's girl friend
   Never needs to work.

A woman who loves to dance
   Is always dreaming.
Whoever marries a dandy
   Does not need to work.

The city's police and courts caused the TMC more serious problems. Although the police often patrolled picket lines and escorted strikebreakers through mill gates during the strike's first month, they seldom interfered with the TMC picket lines. As the crowds grew larger, showing increasing support for the TMC, the police moved in. They made their first arrests on May 10, charging Christina Simores and Angelina Tsoupreas with disturbing the peace, carrying concealed weapons (two feet of gas pipe and a bag of bricks), and attacking a police officer. Tsoupreas had bitten the policeman on the arm when he tried to throw her into the paddy wagon.[3]

"Pickets Admit Their Weapons." Christina Simores (left) and Angelina Tsoupreas, in front of the Pemaquid Mill, were the first pickets arrested. Tsoupreas holds a bag of bricks in her right hand. The prosecutor told the court that the women were "cursing, swearing and using abusive language." When their attorney argued that the women didn't speak English, Judge Milliken said, "Hasn't it been your experience that the first thing foreigners learn is to swear?"
Ashley Scrapbook, Times

Judge Milliken found both women guilty and sentenced them to six months in prison. The women appealed to superior court, and all charges except disturbing the peace were thrown out. Each woman was ordered to spend one month in prison.[4]

More arrests quickly followed. At the end of May, the Citizens' Mediation Committee convinced the mill owners to meet with the Textile Council to discuss a compromise. Nothing came from the meeting because the mill owners continued to insist on the wage cut. But the TMC, excluded from the negotiations, stepped up picketing to convince both the mill owners and the Council that the strike couldn't be settled without them. The police responded by arresting several picketers, including Beal and Murdoch, for disturbing the peace. They were charged with singing on the picket line and encouraging others to sing. Each was found guilty and sentenced to 90 days in prison by Judge Milliken, who further ruled that using the word "scab" was illegal. The TMC appealed all sentences to superior court.

June proved a busy month for the courts as police increased their vigilance. After he was promoted to police chief upon the sudden death of Chief Cole, McLeod directed all policemen to picket duty, postponed vacations and ordered double shifts.[5] On June 14, Elizabeth Donnelly was arrested for singing, "We'll catch the boss and put him in the sauce and never let him go," to the tune of "A hunting we will go."[6] Several others were arrested that day, including Bessie Katsikaras, for the second time. She replied in court, "God gave me my voice, and God is the only one that can keep me quiet."[7] Augusto Pinto, arrested for the third time in the strike, claimed he wasn't singing but was silently opening and closing his mouth.[8] Milliken gave heavy sentences to all three.

TMC pickets under arrest at the Sharp Mill. Police rented trucks to haul strikers to jail. By the end of the strike, police had made about one thousand arrests.
UPI / Bettmann

"Police Quell Pickets in North End." *300 pickets, led by William Murdoch, try to stop strikebreakers from entering Nonquitt Mill. Police are rushing towards the group of pickets.*

Ashley Scrapbook: Evening Standard

The rainy summer gave the TMC another weapon besides singing. While leading a large picket line at the Wamsutta Mill on a rainy morning, Beal was ordered by police to stop singing. Beal replied, "Go to hell," and a policeman moved in to arrest him. A women next to Beal hit the policeman with her umbrella, and a brawl began. The strikers used stones and umbrellas and at least one policeman swung his club. Several people were injured, including Beal and a policeman who was bitten just above the elbow. Beal and eight other strikers were arrested and taken away in paddy wagons. Some 200 picketers followed them on foot, singing and

"3000 Strikers on Guard at Nonquitt Gates Today." *The TMC held large picket lines almost every day until District Court Judge Milliken ruled mass picketing illegal. In 1927, the U. S. Supreme Court upheld a law that imposed a six-month sentence for intimidating strikebreakers. Milliken eventually ruled that almost any picket line activity was illegal.*

Ashley Scrapbook: Times

Pickets at the Pemaquid Mill on Belleville Avenue. On the day the TMC picketed the Nonquit Mill, the Pemaquid did not try to open its gates.

Ashley Scrapbook

"Picket Line Leaders Beg For Arrest". Jack Gomes and Mary Costa heading a TMC picket line in front of the Whitman Mill. Miss Costa, who was 17, cried when she was not arrested after police took three vans of prisoners to jail.

Ashley Scrapbook

shouting. En route, Katsikaras was arrested again but continued to sing at the top of her lungs. When told to keep still at the station, she replied, "Go to hell. I'll picket tomorrow, and I'd like to see the damned cop who can take me out of the picket line."[9]

I worked in the strike as a police officer, working for six months, many times extra hours that we never got paid for. We got three days at the end of six months, three days of compensation for all the hours that we put in during the strike. We were probably 100 to 200 cops, and we had all kinds of big trucks, and none of them resisted very much the arrests. They were told that they couldn't parade, and we took them down to headquarters. They paid their two dollars and were released for appearance later in court. As I say, it didn't amount to nothing. It came for a while to be a very dreary affair because it was the same routine every day.

— Joseph Levesque

I never saw a black cop. Very few Portuguese cops. They were mostly Irish, English, some French Canadians. They were out to break the picket line. There were mass arrests.

— Joe Figueiredo

On June 22, Murdoch, Beal, and 11 other defendants appeared in superior court on appeal from their district court convictions. Murdoch, the first defendant, had been convicted of disturbing the peace by singing after the police had asked the picketers to stop. The prosecution's main witness was Tibbie Kasen, a young woman arrested with Murdoch and Beal, who testified that Murdoch had told the picketers to continue singing. When questioned by Harry Hoffman, the defendant's lawyer, however, she replied she had made up a song which attacked the police and that Murdoch asked her not to sing it because "the police were there to do their duty and would do them no harm."[10]

Crowds gather to insure solidarity.
"This scene outside the Wamsutta at 7 o'clock this morning is typical of what happened at many mill gates, for some seven thousand were out early to make sure that no one should go to work if any of the mills should try to open. The Nonquitt alone made the attempt, and this was a complete failure."

Ashley Scrapbook: Times

When Hoffman questioned the size of the disturbance, Judge Albert Avery instructed the jury, "It was not incumbent on the government to produce a single citizen to say he was disturbed. The commonwealth proves its case if it proves that what was done was such that it would tend to cause such a disturbance as to amount to a nuisance."[11] The English and French-Canadian jury, which probably thought the TMC a nuisance to begin with, convicted Murdoch. Avery sentenced him to 60 days in jail, and five minutes later Murdoch found himself in prison.

The next day, Beal pleaded guilty for a lesser sentence of 30 days in prison. The judge continued the cases of ten other defendants until November. He also dropped the charges against Kasen because she had been a government witness.

The mill owners didn't gain much advantage with Murdoch and Beal in the county jail, however. Angered by the arrests, more people joined the TMC's picket lines; even Textile Council members joined TMC pickets for the first time.

On June 18, Batty and Beal had led rival groups at the Pemaquid Mill. Beal tried to walk in the Council's line, but Council pickets crossed the street to avoid him. On the day of Murdoch's trial, the rival unions picketed together at the Wamsutta gates. At the same spot where he had punched Beal in the face two months earlier, Batty joined him on the picket line, saying, "I am glad to see this group so well organized. What we need is organization to win this strike. I'm going to lead my group in too."[12] The pickets sang and shouted while the police stood quietly on the sidelines and made no arrests.

Later that day, Jacob Minkin, one of New Bedford's leading trial lawyers, appeared in court for the arraignment of Frances Mikolajczyk and Veronica Ogozalak for throwing stones while marching in a Textile

William Murdoch behind bars. Almost all of the 1,000 arrested were found guilty by Judge Milliken and given lengthy sentences. Only four convictions were upheld in Superior Court.

Ashley Scrapbook

Strawberry Jam, Cream of Tartar
Who's the TMC's greatest Martyr
Murdoch, Murdoch, hail, hail, hail
He got 60 days in jail

Attorney Jacob Minkin, Judge Frank Milliken and Police Chief Samuel McLeod. Minkin was New Bedford's leading labor and civil rights lawyer for 25 years after the strike. In 1931 he ran for U.S. Representative as a socialist. Milliken, the son of a mill owner, was district court judge for over 30 years before the strike. Several mill owners were clients of Milliken's law firm. McLeod became chief when William Cole died at the beginning of the strike.
Standard-Times, Ashley Scrapbook

Council picket line at the Wamsutta Mill. At their trial a few days later, Minkin carefully distinguished his defendants from the TMC, referring to the "slander and calumny being heaped upon New Bedford because of the activities of outsiders." He convinced Special Judge James Doran that the police had no evidence that Mikolajczyk had thrown any stones. Doran found her not guilty, the first acquittal of the strike. He found Ogozalak guilty but filed the case and took care to distinguish her from the TMC pickets, saying she "doesn't appear dangerous or in any way undesirable. She was on the scene and was carried away by the excitement."[13]

Although Minkin never represented the TMC in court, his appearance in the strike stopped the most flagrant abuses of justice. Singing no longer was considered disturbing the peace.

Changing of the guard in the TMC

Since the beginning of the strike, leadership had been shifting away from Beal and Murdoch and towards the Passaic group that was more experienced in leading strikes. Their abrupt transfer from the picket line to making reed-backed chairs in the New Bedford House of Correction simply concluded the change in the TMC's leadership.

Internal fighting over relief money led to the removal of Ann Craton, then head of the TMC relief effort. She was popular among local TMC leaders, and several resigned in protest.

Eli Keller, veteran of the Passaic strike and president of Passaic UTW Local 1618, took Craton's place as head of relief and over the next few weeks assumed control of the TMC. He refused official designation as the TMC's leader in order to avoid expulsion from the UTW, the rival union. The Passaic group of Keller, Rubenstein, and Ellen Dawson, Secretary-Treasurer of another Passaic UTW local, along with occasional visits from Weisbord, now held control of the TMC. When Beal and Murdoch, returned from prison, they worked under the direction of Keller and the others.

The new leadership of the TMC moved even closer to the tactics used in Passaic. They planned a massive parade for July 1 and applied for a city

Eli Keller, Ann Craton and Ellen Dawson.
All three were veterans of the 1926 Passaic strike. Craton was a writer who came to New Bedford to direct relief efforts for the TMC. She wanted all donations used for strike relief, whereas Fred Beidenkapp, president of the WIR, wanted some for organizing costs. They reached a compromise but Albert Weisbord, leader of the Passaic group, accused Craton of working for the mill owners. Stung by the criticism, Craton left the city, and Keller replaced her.
Ashley Scrapbook

permit. Chief McLeod refused on the grounds that the parade was a demonstration. Looking to test the police, the TMC continued with its plans. Keller said he was worried more about the weather than about the police. Sure enough, it rained the day of the parade, but thousands of TMC supporters prepared to march in two groups: one in the North End under Rubenstein, the other in the South End under Keller. They planned to meet in the city's center. McLeod called out every police officer in the city. The police blocked both routes with trucks and paddy wagons and arrested Rubenstein, Keller and 30 others.[14]

You know the sign, "Here we come, 10,000 strong" that we were going to march with. Workers gathered, and we started to march. No sooner had we started when the cops came in with clubs. I've never seen clubs like that size before. They were like Indian route sticks. Have you ever seen the pictures? About three-and-a-half to four feet long. You couldn't get near the guy that was swinging it at you. They waded in to us and broke it up, and that is when I landed in a pie wagon or a converted truck used as a paddy wagon.

I see those clubs in my nightmares. I've never seen clubs like that before or since.

— Jack Rubenstein

Start of TMC parade in South End at Saulnier's lot. Police blocked the route several blocks ahead.
Ashley Scrapbook

The TMC leaders declared that the arrests violated their constitutional right to peaceful assembly. Mayor Ashley defended Chief McLeod, saying, "If the recognized unions want to hold a parade, I will see that they have a permit. They are a splendid group of citizens, and I know they will do nothing contrary to the law. I do oppose and will continue to oppose any parade sponsored by the group of outsiders, who have come in here since the strike began."[15] Special District Court Judge George Gardiner found all defendants guilty of parading without a permit and sentenced them to six months in prison, which they appealed.[16]

"Here We Come! Thousands Strong Behind Us." TMC parade in the North End just before marchers were stopped by police blockade.

Ashley Scrapbook

The strategy borrowed from Passaic worked. For ten weeks, picket lines, parades, rallies and court cases kept the mill workers focused on the strike. Although Textile Council leaders considered mass marches and parades beyond the limits of responsible union behavior, they resumed picketing and even seemed willing to join the TMC on the picket line. Together, at least temporarily, they faced the greatest test of the strike.

The mill owners, who had sold off their inventories and were ready to resume production, prepared to open their gates in a direct confrontation with both the Council and the TMC.

THE MILL OWNERS REOPEN THE MILLS

On June 27, the mill owners announced they would open the mills on Monday, July 9, with the ten percent cut in effect. The Council was confident that the strikers could again shut down the mills. Batty said, "We welcome the test. We have no fear that it will result in anything except a more convincing demonstration than ever of the determination of the textile operatives of New Bedford to stick it out until they win their strike."[17] Both the TMC and the Textile Council prepared for the opening by building their picket lines. On Monday, the week before the opening,

"Raymond Costa, Already a Leader... Led a group of children in the South End parade."

Ashley Scrapbook: Times

the Council held a practice picket. Thousands of mill workers watched large lines from both unions picket the mostly closed mill gates.

Tension mounted as the day for the mill opening approached. Mayor Ashley called in police from other cities and asked for volunteers from the National Guard, offering $5 per day, roughly the same as mill wages for men. When no one volunteered, Ashley conscripted the guard members to serve at the army rate of $1 per day.[18] The National Guard readied mounted soldiers, artillery and live cartridges.

Among the first arrested for parading without a permit. "Mrs. Rose Fernandes holds on to her daughter as she was placed under arrest and hustled away into an awaiting truck by Patrolmen Edward T. McDermott and Archie A. Sylvia." Seventeen thousand dollars in bonds was pledged for 28 arrests.

Ashley Scrapbook

A couple of times before the sellout, the mill owners made efforts to open up the mills, and they called out the National Guard. I was in Battery F. They called out the riot call, and we all went up to the state armory. We were all lined up. Now in Battery F most of us had friends or members of our families who were on strike, and some of us were strikers. So that when they called out the batteries, the one battery they didn't call was Battery F. And just as we were changing into military clothes in the armory I was talking with the guys in the locker room. One guy says, "I ain't going to shoot no striker. My mother is on strike." I was already known as being an activist in the strike. So I'm talking with this guy, Ted, and I said, "If they send us out there what are we going to do?" There was this lieutenant who was about 30 feet away who overheard the conversation in the locker room. So when they were up in front to call out the batteries, they sent out Battery B, the cavalry. But we were kept in the armory. Later on we learned that they had decided that there were too many people in Battery F that they could not rely on.

— Joe Figueiredo

Police loading parade leaders into trucks. "Thousands of spectators applauded as strikers marched in the face of police warning. Many joined in the hand to hand fighting, kicking and scuffling. Twenty-eight persons fell into police nets and were charged with rioting and parading without a permit."

Ashley Scrapbook

"Open Gates Prove Uninviting... A scene typical of morning developments. An open gate at the Wamsutta with a picket line barring the portal and no one attempting to go to work." No one crossed the picket line when the mill owners tried to re-open the mills in the 12th week of the strike.
Ashley Scrapbook

MOUNTED SOLDIERS HOLD INTEREST OF WATCHING THRONGS

Opening of Gates Attended by 20,000 Pickets and Spectators—Batty Avers Tieup Complete

New Bedford's mills opened their gates today for the first time in 12 weeks. Machinery long silent clacked and whirred and throbbed invitingly through open windows; mill whistles tooted at the accustomed hours—but practically no one went to work except

On July 9, 20,000 mill workers picketed the mill gates and watched as almost no one entered the mills. A jubilant Batty declared, "A complete tie-up. We have won for the second time. It is wonderful. Never has there been such a display of solidarity in a textile strike before. The crowds just cheered and applauded when the gates were closed at 7:15. You would have thought it a vaudeville show rather than a strike."[19]

Mayor Ashley and Chief McLeod claimed credit for peace on the picket lines and justified their use of National Guard troops. Ashley, still trying to placate both the mill owners and the Textile Council, said, "Our people here are not troublesome and never have been. It was not because of any action on their part that the National Guardsmen were brought into the situation, but there are outsiders here who would cause trouble if they could, and I know it."[20]

I don't know what it was but it was not a typical strike. Well, for one thing the scab problem never was very big down there. That was one of the

National Guard preparing for duty. The Passaic veterans in the TMC, who had faced armed National Guardsmen several times in that strike, were not flustered by the militia. Rubenstein said, *"Militiamen cannot weave cloth; they may have a moral effect, but they cannot break the strike."* Batty and the other Council leaders feared that the National Guard would cause problems. They asked that the militia use only trained horses. *"The aim of the Textile Council is to close the mills once more without the raising of a police club, knowing as we do that when a police club is raised it is always the worker's head that suffers."*
Ashley Scrapbook

"Pickets and Onlookers Boo as Nonquitt Strikebreakers Are Whisked Away." Day by day, crowds of strikers gathered at the entrance gates to loudly jeer as strikebreakers were "whisked" into work. "Only 38 operatives went to work at the Nonquitt yesterday, police report, five less than the day before. The crowd booed loudly when they were rushed out in cars yesterday afternoon, as this picture shows. Today only 12 were counted going in by the police."

Ashley Scrapbook: Times

main reasons probably why it was relatively peaceful. There were a few instances where the scabs did break through, but the problem never became big enough for wholesale violence. I'm sure that if it did, there would have been resistance.

— Frank Manning

Both the TMC and the Textile Council intensified their picket lines after the mill reopened. On July 10, several thousand TMC supporters picketed all night at the Kilburn Mill, which was rumored to be operating with strikebreakers.

It was reported that some scabs had been taken in by some mill owners, and we kept a 24-hour picket line going for a little over two days. The interesting thing is that the fishermen helped us. You see, the Kilburn Mill was right on the water, and the fishermen helped us with their boats so the result was that after two-and-a-half days, the owner had to let the scabs out.

— Eula Mendes

"Some of the 12,000 Who Gathered to Watch the Kilburn Siege." "The scabs couldn't come out because they were afraid of us, and it was very difficult for food to go into them."

Ashley Scrapbook: Mendes

Both unions ran picket lines, with Batty often leading the Council's lines himself. Chief McLeod called out all his men and ordered in some reserves. At times the crowds surged out of control, and on one evening several hundred mill windows were broken.

I was aware of it when it started, but I had nothing to do with it. Not that I would have objected at the time. Maybe I would have, I don't know, because stoning the buildings and breaking the windows is not my cup of tea. I realize nothing good can come of that.

— Jack Rubenstein

The police and the courts' more permissive stance towards the Council began to change. Chief McLeod stood by the arrests of four Council members for picketing strikebreakers' homes, saying, "People have an unquestionable right to go to and from their homes and what is further to live in their homes, without being disturbed by anyone."[21] For the first time in the strike, New Bedford's Board of Commerce openly opposed the Textile Council and unanimously voted that, "mass and house picketing and the formation of crowds in the vicinity of industrial plants act against the best interest of the whole community, and the board appeals to the public to discourage the continuance of such practices and to support the authorities in a strict enforcement of the law."[22]

The Council, which was a member of the Board of Commerce, sharply disagreed.[23] Batty said, "The Board apparently regards the strike as a picnic, but it is more than that. It is a struggle for existence, an economic right, and we will not yield our legal rights and privileges."[24]

The TMC and the Textile Council won the battle on the picket lines and kept the mills from operating. For a few days, the city's newspapers

Police Chief McLeod at his desk. McLeod had been on the police force for over 30 years. He had climbed the ranks from patrolman to police chief.

Standard-Times

Picket line at home of strikebreaker. Both the TMC and the Textile Council picketed strikebreakers' homes. Sometimes the TMC went further. "This lady is still alive today and her husband was a businessman. He made her go to work, and they used to tell her not to go because she was going to be in trouble. But she said that she had to go to work because her husband told her to go. One day, a bunch of women got hold of her and took off all her clothes. I felt bad for the woman because she was really naked and someone came along and threw a coat over her. From that day on that lady never went back to work."

Evening Standard: Alves

reported the numbers going into the mills to work. But this tactic, which in previous strikes had enticed more people into the mills as the numbers rose, failed because the newspapers reported that fewer, not more, people were entering the mills. After three months on strike, the workers were as determined as ever, and the rival unions were solidly united, at least in closing the mills.[25] The mill owners realized that they would have to do more than simply open the mill gates.

They decided to attack.

THE MILL OWNERS VS. THE TEXTILE COUNCIL AND THE TMC

The week after they failed to reopen the mills, the mill owners changed leaders. Andrew Raeburn, the executive secretary of the Manufacturers' Association, claimed illness and took a vacation from the city; and John Sullivan, president of the Association and owner of the Taber Mill, took charge.

Sullivan immediately claimed that picketing deprived the mill owners and workers of their right to reopen the mills. He announced, "We believe that there are thousands of people who would like to work if they were not intimidated by strike pickets and their sympathizers. If the strikers are so confident as they profess to be that nobody wants to return to work, let them withdraw their pickets."[26] The always unflappable Binns replied, "We might suggest in return that the Manufacturers' Association dissolve their combine and see what would happen if each was free to go ahead on his own."[27]

Sullivan saved most of his criticism for the TMC, which he said "constitutes a menace both to the mills and to the established labor organizations. It is directly connected to the communistic and bolshevik organizations and lives on trouble."[28] Sullivan also declared there were 800 "reds" in New Bedford and charged that Quakers, Republican congressmen and some clergymen had joined the socialists.

Sullivan also blamed the police, Mayor Ashley and the courts for being too lenient. He advised Mayor Ashley to emulate former governor Calvin Coolidge, who had fired all the striking police in Boston ten years earlier. He also told the court to limit the number of people on picket lines and at other gatherings to the "smallest possible number."[29]

Some mill owners decided to take direct action themselves. The same day that Sullivan started his attack, John Burton, owner and general manager at the Nashawena Mill, got out of his car at a picket line and threatened the crowd with his revolver. The police stepped in and convinced him to get back into his car. Burton had said earlier at a public meeting that "he wants every Red run out of town."[30]

Chief McLeod asked Mayor Ashley to hire more police officers, and he cancelled almost all vacations. Both men pressured District Attorney William Crossley to schedule special superior court sessions to hear district court appeals, but Crossley eventually decided against a special session.

John Sullivan, president of the Manufacturers' Association. Sullivan objected to editorials and public opinion in favor of the strike and the mayor's leniency. He criticized the newspapers for publishing pictures of huge crowds around the mill gates. "The very presence of these people in these places is contrary to law, for in numbers such as that they constitute intimidation which has no warrant in the law, nor in equity either."
Standard-Times

MILLIKEN DECLARES STRIKE'S ACTIVITIES BECOMING NUISANCE

Asserts Crowds Make Intimidation— 'Keep Away from Mills,' Advises Court, Continuing Cases

Bringing his fist down with a bang on the bench, answering a whispered question from Harry Hoffman, counsel for a dockful of Textile Workers union defendants in Third District Court today, Judge Frank A. Milliken, in an emphatic voice, said: "No!

MISS REISCH HELD
WITH FIVE OTHERS
IN LINE AT SHARP

Dispute Over Space Near Mill Gate Results in Arrest of Pinto for Sixth Time
—Extra Patrolmen Called to Scene

A disturbance at the Sharp mill this morning resulted in six
arrests of pickets, among them, Miss Sadie Reisch, special women's
organizer for the New Bedford Textile council. Miss Reisch is the
first Textile council leader arrested since the strike began.

A few days after Sullivan requested that the police stop the picketing, both the Council and the TMC sent large picket lines to stop strikebreakers from entering the Sharp Mill. Sergeant Augustus Velho told picket leaders to disband their picket lines. When the TMC refused, Velho arrested several picketers, including Augusto Pinto, for parading without a permit. A scuffle ensued because members of both unions liked Pinto, and Velho told Reisch, who was leading the Council's picket, to disband her line. She stood her ground, and Velho put her in the police wagon. Reisch was the first Council leader arrested in the strike.

Picket Line at the Sharp Mill. Police took names of strikers so that warrants could be issued if the court determined the picketing illegal. Police were called to the Sharp Mill when followers of Pinto became "noisy and demonstrative" following his arrest. Police then ordered the lines to disperse but Sadie Reisch stood her ground, saying, "I didn't want to be arrested, but I did want to stand on my rights."

Ashley Scrapbook

In a prepared statement, Batty criticized Mayor Ashley and Chief McLeod for the arrests. "The arrests this morning for parading without a permit at the Sharp mill is a far cry from the mayor's public statement that the Textile Council could parade any time they wanted with a police escort." Batty compared Reisch's arrest for peaceful picketing with the police force's condoning Burton's drawing a gun on the picketers. "This difference in treatment by the police department is due to the existence of an invisible government," he said.[31]

Chief McLeod answered, "The orders issued at the Sharp did not indicate any change in policy, but were given in accordance with standing orders issued several weeks ago to the police department. This will put it up to the courts to decide whether those taken into custody were parading or picketing."[32]

Abraham Binns, William Batty and Horace Riviere lead Textile Council picket line at the Sharp Mill the day after the police arrested Sadie Reisch for parading without a permit. Pinto was arrested for the sixth time. Over 1,200 pickets from both the TMC and the Textile Council marched together.

Ashley Scrapbook

"Police Capture Struggling Pickets in Sharp Mill Roundup."
Ashley Scrapbook

The next day, a police force of more than 100 was dispatched to the Sharp Mill to break up a crowd of over five thousand picketers from the TMC. When the police moved in to arrest Pinto again, a riot broke out. Several police officers were injured, including Sergeants William H. McCarty, veteran of many a struggle with pickets, and Augustus Velho, who had made most of the arrests in the strike. McCarty was bitten on the arm, hit on the head with a large stone and pummeled with fists and clubs. McLeod gave the order to read the riot act, which meant that everyone present could be arrested for rioting, and the crowd disbanded. It was the first time in McLeod's 33 years on the police force that the riot act had been read in the city. Eight people were arrested, most for assaulting officers.

In court the next morning, Milliken pounded his fist on the bench and declared, "No! Picketing in New Bedford has got to stop. It is a nuisance entirely. These people must keep away from the mills entirely. They have no business there."[33] That afternoon, anticipating more distur-

"Order is Everyone Get a Man... One of the struggles that occurred as excited prisoners battled with their captors."
Ashley Scrapbook

"*When riot at the Sharp Mill was at its height.* Sergeants McCarty and Velho grapple with strikers while one TMC picket is shown seizing a policeman's leg in an attempt to throw him.

Ashley Scrapbook

They bought McCarty for 50 cents,
  Parlez-vous.
They bought McCarty for 50 cents,
  Parlez-vous.
They bought McCarty for 50 cents
  The son of a bitch he jumped the fence,
Inky-dinky parlez-vous.

bances, McLeod sent to Fall River for police reinforcements. Again, the riot act was read to the throngs of strikers at the Sharp Mill. When the crowd failed to disperse, strikers were herded into awaiting vans. Eighty-two were arrested and charged with rioting.

Over the next few weeks, Milliken kept his promise to stop the picketing. He reduced the maximum picket size to ten people and then to one person. He gave harsher sentences and larger fines and increased bail for disturbing the peace to more than a mill worker's yearly salary. TMC members and their supporters continued to pledge cash and property to bail out those arrested, however.[34] Over half a million dollars was raised for bail, mostly from New Bedford's Portuguese community.[35]

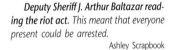

Deputy Sheriff J. Arthur Baltazar reading the riot act. This meant that everyone present could be arrested.

Ashley Scrapbook

Walking the line. Keller and Amy Schechter lead TMC picket line; Batty gets arrested at the Whitman Mill; and Kaczor leads Textile Council picket line.

Ashley Scrapbook

There were some very vicious battles. For instance, the mill owners got a judge to minimize the picketing. Our committee's answer to that was mass picketing. So I was directed to the Hathaway Mill. We had about one thousand pickets there. That day there were about 45 people arrested. And some people were hurt. There was this Portuguese worker. They cracked his head. They took him down to the police station which was about ten blocks away. They had thousands of people around that police station trying to get him out.

— Joe Figueiredo

Altogether, there was something like 888 arrests, and many of them were arrested many times. For example, I was arrested a number of times, I don't know how many times. We sometimes stayed just a few hours, sometimes overnight or sometimes even days or weeks, but we were usually let out on bail. And a few days later maybe we were arrested again.

— Eula Mendes

Although the court's ire was directed mostly at the TMC, the police's heavy hand also fell on the Textile Council for the first time in the strike. Reisch was arrested several times after her initial arrest for parading without a permit at the Sharp Mill, and other Council leaders, including Kaczor, Riviere, Thompson and Manning, were arrested and received jail sentences from Milliken. Eventually, Reisch and Kaczor were evicted from

Attorney Jacob Minkin on the steps of 3rd District Court with William Batty and other Textile Council defendants. Frank Manning and "Red Mike" Shulman are on the far right. Shulman said that he walked from New York to New Bedford to work for the Textile Council.

Ashley Scrapbook

their lodgings at the YWCA because of their arrests, raising an outcry from clergymen and from YWCA members who worked in the mills.[36]

> *Sadie Reisch and Josephine Kaczor lived at the YWCA, which was dominated by the millmen's wives' association. And they came to Sadie and to Josephine, those nice mill women, and said that they were going to ask them to leave because of their strike activities. That night we had a big meeting, and I spoke and addressed them and said. "Let's rechristen the YWCA the Millmen's Wives." I said that throwing these two women out with no definite place to go was one of the crassest things that revealed their true colors as instruments of the mill owners.*
>
> *So Sadie and Josephine got a room, and about two weeks later, two very nice-looking women came to see me from the New York YWCA office. They came to apologize. They said, "We feel that we owe you an apology and, more than that, we would like to do something." I said, "Well, you could make a contribution to the strike fund." And they did.*
>
> — Frank Manning

Finally, even Batty was arrested for loitering when he walked the picket lines. Because there weren't enough police wagons to take all the prisoners, Batty drove himself and three companions to the station.[37]

Its allies continued to support the Textile Council. The city's newspapers still opposed the wage cut and even editorialized against Milliken's ban on picketing.[38] Relief funds continued to flow from the city's professional and business people, keeping open the soup kitchens. The UTW and other unions including the AFTO, which the Council had quit at the start of the strike, continued relief collections. The Citizens Mediation Committee still looked for a way out of the strike.

Rubenstein and Beal arrested.
Courtesy of Jack Rubenstein

Much of the city's clergy stuck with the strikers. Rev. Linden White, pastor of St. Martin's Episcopal Church, reported to the newspapers that he had been approached by a private detective hired by the mill owners, who had asked him to urge his parishioners to return to work. Rev. White said that the agent also had visited Father Henry J. Noon, pastor of St. James' Catholic Church and a member of the Citizens Mediation Committee, but that Father Noon also had refused to preach his congregation back to work. A few days after the visit, Father Noon sent a letter to the city's newspapers, which they printed on the front page, telling mill workers, "Never go back under this cut," and asking the mill owners, "Be big, take down your notices of a cut and then and not till then, open your gates."[39]

While the Textile Council increased its picketing, the TMC continued to lead the mass pickets, facing constant hostility from the police and the courts. When the TMC applied to Mayor Ashley for another parade permit, he again refused and brought in another small army of police and militia. Once again it rained, but this time the TMC backed down and called off the march.

"Trouble Brews in Textile Strike Zone." The TMC waits at Saulnier's lot for the parade to start. Ashley had refused the TMC a permit, and the police were ready to arrest the marchers. But it started raining before the parade could begin.
UPI / Bettmann

Truckload of TMC members taken to jail. Augusto Pinto is raising his fist. "There is no liberty in this country, just a statue," Pinto told a Times reporter.
Ashley Scrapbook: Times

On July 30, several police vans pulled up to the Whitman Mill and began arresting people on the picket line. Beal, fresh from his 30-day prison term, encouraged everyone to climb into the vans.[40] The police, rather than push people into the vans, were busy pulling women and children out.

> *People were hungry. I remember one time there was a march and the police brought those big moving vans. Everybody jumped into the vans to get arrested just to get a full meal. That was quite a stunt!*
>
> — Al Saulnier

The final count was 256 people arrested, a record for the strike.[41] More bedlam followed at the police station. Defendants appeared by the score before Milliken, who sentenced Beal, Rubenstein and the other leaders to six months in jail and the rest to two months.

"Kinfolk of Jailed Picketers Wait Wearily for Chance to Bail Them Out... This photograph was taken in front of the police station several hours after the National Guard had driven back the crowd."
Ashley Scrapbook: Times

Meanwhile, a huge crowd of strikers and their families surrounded the police station.[42] McLeod called out the National Guard, which drove back the crowds with fixed bayonets. Several strikers didn't retreat and were thrown into jail with the others. A few people were cut by bayonets or bruised by the crowds. Like most confrontations during the strike, however, even with hundreds of heavily armed militia and police, the scene resembled a carnival more than it did a pitched battle. For the next few days, the jails remained full and hundreds of people crowded around the police station, but the militia backed off and the situation cooled. Eventually, all those arrested were released on bail.

"Preparing 256 Court Cases." Chief McLeod and Deputy Chief Raymond Chase of Fall River *"at work checking on the wholesale arrests last night. All have their hands full of arrest cards."*

Ashley Scrapbook

I remember one occasion when we had a huge meeting in New Bedford and the mayor became worried and called out the National Guard. During that day, several strikers had been arrested and were put in jail. It seemed that the court ruled that the picket line had to be held down to four persons. Mr. Thompson and I hadn't read that, and when we came out of our rooms, there were only four picketers and I said to Don, "What goes on here? Where is everybody?" So we walked over and got in back of the pickets and started conversation, and the first thing I knew I was in the patrol wagon with Don Thompson.

So along with a couple of hundred others, we were jailed all day. At night, seven thousand strikers gathered outside of the jail demanding our

"Pickets Become Prisoners." Police and National Guard load another truck with picketers to be taken to the police station. Over 250 people were arrested, and the jail was surrounded by guardsmen with bayonets drawn when a crowd of several thousand people gathered there.

UPI / Bettmann

"Jack Rubenstein sticks his head out of the van of prisoners to exhort his followers to come on in and be arrested." National Guardsman on horseback.
Ashley Scrapbook

GUARDSMEN SHOW BAYONETS, SPREAD CROWD IN STREET

Battery of 80 Scatters 10,000 Persons Who Gather at Station After Arrest of 256

ORDERED OUT BY CHIEF McLEOD

Soldiers Leave Armory as Crowd Grows About Headquarters—Trucks Bring Pickets in to Be Booked

A force of 80 National Guardsmen fixed bayonets and drove 10,000 persons away from the central police station late last night after the arrest and imprisonment there of 256 pickets from the Whitman and Kilburn mills.

release. And they were facing this huge audience with drawn guns and bayonets. It was really something.

— Frank Manning

I still remember the day the National Guard came down in trucks and put all those people in them and brought them all down to the police station. That's the only time my father said, "C'mon, we have to go down and see it." And we did. The whole city of New Bedford was there. They wanted to see if they could break the picket lines and try to break the union, but they couldn't. Five hundred people down at the police station in the center and you could hear them inside screaming, and you could hear them on the outside.

I'll never forget that day. The National Guard came down with their bayonets and tried to get the people to go home. I got scared and ran away. I'll never forget for I broke my heel while running. My father got scared when he saw the bayonets. They let people out of jail the next day, and these people went back on the picket line. Nobody got hurt, but the bayonets did scare people.

— Mary Alves

The TMC was not as successful in spreading the strike to Fall River, the neighboring textile city. After two months of battling Chief Martin Feeney

Fall River TMC group pays a visit to New Bedford.
Ashley Scrapbook

James Reid exhorts crowd, "One More Fall River Arrest," and "Outside Home of Drowned Boy." Reid was a Providence RI dentist, long involved in communist labor organizing, who had served in the Rhode Island legislature. During a police confrontation at a picket line a six-year old boy drowned in a small pond nearby. The TMC claimed that the boy drowned because the police drove the crowd into the pond. Chief Martin Feeney answered that witnesses said that the boy had been swimming for about an hour before he drowned and that his clothes were found on the shore.

Ashley Scrapbook

over the right to hold meetings and rallies, the TMC called a strike against the Fall River mill owners, who had cut wages six months earlier. On August 9, several hundred workers walked out of the American Printing Company and the Lincoln and Algonquin mills. Beal led the picket lines, and five thousand TMC supporters gathered in front of the print works.[43] John Campos, the UTW leader in Fall River, urged workers not to join the strike, but the crowd booed him, and the police had to help him into his car to escape.[44] The police made several arrests, breaking up the rally.

District Court Judge Edward Hanify was particularly harsh with the TMC. When the 100 or so arrested appeared in court, he gave Rubenstein, James Reid and the other leaders six months in jail. He offered the rank and file probation, but only if they denounced the TMC.[45]

I was thrown into the paddy wagon and taken to jail. I could hear some fighting and arguments upstairs. I could tell by what was going on, the door being banged, that somebody was being beaten up and these two policemen

"Organizer is Choked into Submission. Peter Hagelias is Arrested... When Fall River police seized this TMC organizer near the American Printing Company last night he is said to have shouted, 'Come on boys, get after them.'"

UPI / Bettmann

"Group of Liberty Girls in South End TMC March." Mary Costa dressed as Liberty. At right, the Bristol Mill unit marches in the North End division of the TMC parade.
Ashley Scrapbook

began dragging this drunk down about 40 stairs. He was argumentative, but nothing that happened there warranted this kind of treatment. They would have done this to anyone else that went to jail. That was the relationship of the police and the public at that time, at least the part of the public that went to jail.

— Jack Rubenstein

Hanify set bail of about two years' wages for each of the TMC leaders and for those members who didn't denounce the TMC. A few days later, the Fall River strike ended when most workers drifted back to the mills.

The defeat in Fall River didn't weaken support for the TMC among New Bedford mill workers. On August 21, seven thousand people greeted Murdoch on his release from prison. He gave a speech to over five thousand at Saulnier's lot. A few days later, Mayor Ashley was forced to give the TMC a parade permit for Labor Day because he already had given a parade permit to the Textile Council. He listed several conditions, however: the TMC had to march separately from the Council, and no children, singing, placards and banners, "excepting those bearing name of organization," could be part of the parade.[46]

"Strike Rivals Put Ranks to Test in Parades." Marching from the North End, the TMC followed its usual strategy of two parades, one from each end of the city, meeting in the center. CV Suicidade, Santo Cristo, S. Catolica, S. Continental, Progressive Club and Monte Pio were among the Cape Verdean and Portuguese organizations that marched with the TMC parade
Ashley Scrapbook: Daily Worker

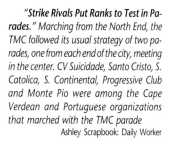

TMC marchers from Nashawena Mill.
During the strike the TMC formed the New Bedford Textile Workers Union, a local of the National Textile Workers Union. At right, "Banners that were barred from the parade. Police banned 'provocative' and 'slogan' banners."

Ashley Scrapbook: Times

On September 9, after a week's postponement due to rain, five thousand union members marched through the city as several thousand more lined the streets and attended the day's events. Council members and their supporters quietly marched behind their union's insignia, and speakers included politicians and celebrities, led by U.S. Senator David Walsh. But the TMC march was several times larger than the Council's and, as usual, more colorful. Many wore traditional Portuguese attire, and scores of marchers carried U.S. flags. To avoid Ashley's prohibition, the TMC had formed organizations such as "The Society of 700 Prisoners," signifying those arrested during the strike, with banners to match.

The next day, the editorial in the *Evening Standard* praised both groups for their decorum. It had the Textile Council firmly in mind, however, when it offered hope "that reason and justice would soon triumph, the essential partnership would be restored, and workers and management would soon unite in operating the industry on which New Bedford's welfare depends."[47]

Women's Trade Union League marches along Pleasant Street in the Textile Council parade. Photograph taken from the Stan-dard-Times building.

Ashley Scrapbook: Evening Standard

"Many tenement houses stand vacant.
The windows are plastered with old newspapers.
A city for rent."

— Moshe Nadir

Strikers' children waiting for food. "The textile strike situation in New Bedford, Mass. is daily growing more serious, and the dire situation of the strikers and their families may precipitate trouble any moment." [UPI/Bettman]

CHAPTER 7

THE SETTLEMENT

At first they said it would not last any longer than two weeks. At first people were in a holiday spirit. Women decided to clean their homes for it was spring – a nice spring. The men were working in their yards as it seemed to me that it wasn't going to last very long, but it lasted. The summer came along and soup kitchens opened up. The bluefish ran in the river, and there was so much fishing that you couldn't get a place on the bridge to fish that year. On Friday we had bluefish in the chowder. Things got pretty bad as the summer went along because now all the money that people had was gone. People weren't paying their rents, and the little stores suffered.
— Gladys Howcroft

Starvation, more than reason and justice, forced the Council's leaders to look for a way out of the strike. Their members had survived the strike's hardships by not paying rent and by eating from their gardens and from the sea, but after six months without paychecks the strikers were desperate; summer was over and winter was coming. Union treasuries were empty and strike collections had slowed to a trickle. Landlords and grocers faced bankruptcy from their extension of credit to the mill workers out on strike.

The Textile Council began courting the mill owners, who also wanted the strike to end because they were losing business to their competitors. U.S. Senator William Butler, Republican National Committee chairman, pressured his fellow mill owners to settle because the national publicity on the strike countered the myth of Republican prosperity during the roaring '20s and could hurt Republican chances in the 1928 national election. However, the mill owners would not give up the wage cut and accept a union victory, which would weaken their hold over factory discipline.

The two groups met sometimes openly, usually with the mediation of third parties, and sometimes secretly, but they always excluded the TMC, whom both regarded as the enemy. Both the Council's leaders and the mill owners saw a settlement as a way to eliminate the TMC. Without the strike, the TMC would have little standing with the mill workers and no legitimate place in the city.

Mediation and Fact–Finding

The Citizens Mediation Committee had arranged a conference between the Textile Council and the Manufacturers' Association at the end of May, but no progress resulted.[1] During the summer, the Committee met with Council leaders and mill owners separately but was unable to bring them together.

On August 8, after both sides rejected binding arbitration of the dispute, the State Board of Conciliation and Arbitration began fact–finding hearings on the strike. The State Board, composed of one representative each from the public, management and labor, could call witnesses and examine company records but could not force either side to accept a settlement. Edward Fisher, chairman of the State Board, preferred arbitration because "even when the Board has filed its report there is no authority back of it other than such public sentiment as it may help create."[2]

The hearings were held in a meeting room in City Hall, where Sullivan and a few of his fellow mill owners sat on one side of a large table facing Batty, Binns, Minkin and other Council leaders. The three Board members, including Mulespinners Union President Samuel Ross, who served as the labor representative on the State Board, sat at the head of the table. No women, Portuguese, Polish, or French–Canadian mill workers sat at the table, nor did any testify at the hearings.

Sullivan began the proceedings by reading a long list of mills that had left New England for the South and argued that the mill owners were simply trying to save New Bedford's industry with the wage cut. He also argued that workers probably would receive more total pay with the wage cut than without it because many mills would have to close if wages weren't cut. However, when pressed by Fisher, Sullivan admitted that more than wage cuts were necessary to cure the industry's problems.

Jacob Minkin and Abraham Binns listen to John Sullivan, representing the mill owners before the State Board of Conciliation. Sullivan refused to respond to the Board's questions. "He had not expected his word to be challenged," wrote the Times, "for he had moved in a world where his ideas were accepted without question. He had shown himself, not the impartial expert he had seemed, but merely a mouthpiece of the feelings rather than the certainties of his employing class."
Ashley Scrapbook

As the strike dragged on month to month, the converters and their customers began to be apprehensive about their sources of supply. It was not very long before more of the better equipped mills in the Carolinas made an effort to break into what for them was a fairly new field. Most of the southern mills had been equipped to manufacture hard and coarser yarn, and consequently, heavier construction such as print cloths, denims and so forth. Therefore, they lacked the combing equipment necessary to comb out the shorter fiber from the longer stapled cut and using finer yarn. It was not very long before the situation was dealt with, and the inexorable drift to the South began.

— William Isherwood

STRIKERS GET FOOD AT AGENCIES, SWIM AND REST IN PARKS

Checkup of Summer's Activities in Ranks of Idle Mill Workers Shows Some at Odd Jobs

COLD DAYS TO BRING PROBLEM

Part of Operatives Have Money in Banks—At Least 1,500 Believed to Have Left New Bedford

This is the 126th day since approximately 27,000 textile operatives struck at 86 plants of 27 corporations and took to their homes
The greater part of them have loafed ever since. What they do

While pickets marched and leaders negotiated, record numbers of bathers swarmed the municipal beaches.
Evening Standard

Batty then testified that the wage cuts were unnecessary, given rising profits, and were "arbitrary and un-American. It is our view that negotiation should have preceded the wage cut. If the operators had wanted our cooperation they could have had it for the asking."[3] Batty also offered "to negotiate with the manufacturers in a thorough study of methods and techniques of management and manufacture with a view to eliminate unnecessary cost."[4]

"Sought Place in Today's Conference." TMC leaders were not given a place at the table when the State Board heard arguments from the mill owners and the Textile Council. Andrew Izyk, treasurer, Eula Mendes, secretary, and Eli Keller, organizer, stand in the front. Behind them are Antone Samiero, Carlos Teizeira, William Markham, Antone Correira, Manuel Pitta, Joseph Talbot and Joseph Vieira.
Ashley Scrapbook

The TMC wasn't given a place at the table, but just before the proceedings ended, Eli Keller was allowed to speak. He accused the Board of operating a sham whose only purpose was to bolster the sagging reputation of the Textile Council, which he claimed was secretly plotting with the mill owners to speed up the line in exchange for the old wage. "Let the real workers come here and testify, not well paid officials who represent a tiny handful of workers," he said.[5] The Board ignored Keller, and Fisher closed the hearing expressing the hope that the parties would come to agreement before the Board had to issue its report.

SPEEDUP OR WAGE CUT OR BOTH

On September 4, the Citizens' Mediation Committee officially proposed to the Council that it accept a speedup in exchange for rescinding the wage cut. Throughout the strike, newspaper editorials, some mill owners, and even Batty had hinted that costs could be reduced without cutting wages. Now Leonard Frieder, the general manager of National

Spun Silk, one of the mills that had not cut wages, suggested a plan to cut costs in the cotton mills by increasing the number of machines each worker operated. On Saturday, September 8, Raeburn and Sullivan, without the other mill owners present, met with the Council's executive committee at the New Bedford Hotel to discuss the plan. Neither side would comment on the meeting's results, but Sullivan was encouraged by "the readiness of the Textile Council to cooperate in the specialization system."[6]

The TMC, again excluded from the meeting, circled the hotel shouting, "No speedup system," with the police in hot pursuit.[7] The TMC argued that a speedup not only would increase work loads but also would cause unemployment because fewer workers would make more cloth.[8] Keller, who had just returned from a long awaited meeting with

TMC Leaders: Eli Keller, William Murdoch, Eula Mendes and Fred Beal.
Standard-Times

Governor Alvin Fuller, predicted that the deal wouldn't go through: "A Fuller/mill-owner/Batty combination exists which the workers cannot penetrate, and this combination is secretly negotiating to sell out the strike. We expect that suddenly the negotiations will be broken off, police activities increased and the extraordinary drive started to get the workers back into the mills under the ten percent cut."[9]

Keller was right. Two days later, after the Council told the Mediation Committee it would accept the cost-cutting plan, the Manufacturers' Association met to consider the proposal. It decided to accept the cost-cutting plan but keep the wage cut, arguing that under specialization the skilled workers could make up for lower piece rates through higher rates of production.

Aware that he had shown his hand too soon and fearful of looking foolish to his members, Batty declared that the speedup combined with the wage cut was "entirely unacceptable" and urged strikers "to renew their energies for waging a successful strike. The strike committee has absolutely no apologies to make to anyone for the present situation."[10] Rubenstein rubbed salt into Batty's wound by telling the newspapers, "Batty turned one cheek, and the manufacturers slammed him on both."[11]

The Textile Council Votes to End the Strike

One week later, the State Board announced it was returning to New Bedford, not to continue its fact-finding but to offer a compromise to end the strike. The board, along with the Citizens Mediation Committee, planned to hold another conference bringing together the Council and the mill owners. Both parties agreed to further negotiations, and at a private meeting of the Council, Ross tried to win them over to the State Board's compromise, rumored to be a five percent cut.

W. C. PRESCOTT URGES STRONGEST MILLS TO WAIVE CUT IN WAGES

SAYS CONTINUED STRIKE MEANS DESTRUCTION

Plants in Position to Adopt Specialization Plan Have Everything to Gain by Settlement, Treasurer of Kidder Company Declares

In a statement to The Standard today William C. Prescott urges that those mills in the New Bedford Cotton Manufacturers'

William C. Prescott, director of the Page Mill and son of Oliver Prescott, president of Wamsutta Mills. Prescott urged mill owners to increase productivity and waive the wage cut. "The cotton industry belongs not to a few, but to every member of this community."
Ashley Scrapbook, Evening Standard

While the mill owners and the Council were preparing for their negotiations, the police kept up the pressure on the TMC. On September 19 at the Page Mill, the police used their clubs against the picketers' stones and umbrellas, and Sergeant Augustus Velho fired several shots. Velho claimed he shot in the air, but the TMC charged that he fired into the crowd, wounding several picketers. Velho also clubbed Frank August, a 62-year-old mill worker walking the picket line. August charged that Velho later took him from his cell at the police station, led him to a small room, told him to take off his glasses, announced, "I'm going to kill you," and beat him senseless.[12] Despite August's wounds and the several different versions that Velho gave to the press and the court, Judge Milliken found August guilty of assault and sentenced him to four months in jail. For the next few mornings after the riot at the Page Mill, thousands of people picketed the mill, but no new fighting broke out.

Frank Augusto, 62, was "clubbed into submission" by Sergeant Augustus Velho (right) and arrested for "rioting, assault and battery" on three policemen during the morning picket at the Page Mill.
Ashley Scrapbook

On September 25, the State Board and the Citizens' Mediation Committee met with the Council and the Manufacturers' Association in City Hall, holding separate sessions with each group. When the State Board offered its compromise of a five percent wage cut, Binns said the Textile Council would not accept it. The Council's French-Canadian organizer Horace Riviere criticized the Board, saying, "If they could stay out and not come here every five minutes and raise hopes in the minds of the manufacturers, we would be pleased."[13]

"State Board Enters Strike Situation." Herbert Wasgatt, representing employers, Edward Fisher, representing the public, Samuel Ross, representing employees. Ross held his seat on the board for over 30 years.
Ashley Scrapbook

The next day, the Manufacturers' Association unanimously agreed to a five percent wage cut. Ross endorsed the compromise, but the other Council leaders preferred a membership vote, which they scheduled for a week later.

They didn't want to have the strike on their hands for so long, They didn't expect it was going to be such a long strike. And the strike had gotten out of control, out of their hands, and they wanted to hold on to it.

— Eula Mendes

In the few days before the vote, the city's three newspapers, which previously had opposed a wage cut, endorsed the compromise. The *Evening Standard* editorialized, "This is not the settlement we had hoped for, but we are forced to the conclusion that unless it is accepted no settlement will be possible."[14] The *Times* also prodded the Council members to vote for the settlement: "The New Bedford textile unions have for all practical purposes won aggressively and honorably (and) should accept the compromise and return to work immediately."[15] The editor of the *Mercury* wrote: "We commend to the mill workers without reservation the acceptance of this compromise. The only alternative, we believe, would be the prolongation of the strike into the dead of winter which would entail great suffering upon thousands of men, women, and children."[16]

What saved a lot of people were their gardens. We had chickens, rabbits and vegetables. A lot of people had their stuff or they would have starved. A lot of people were living on boiled potatoes and carrots, because they had nothing to eat. My father walked from the house all the way to Padanaram pushing a lawn mower by hand to get a quarter an hour. And if there wasn't enough, he'd have to re-mortgage his house because it was paid for, and he had to re-mortgage it more than once so we could eat, because there was nothing else he could do.

— Mary DeRoches

Although they still blamed the mill owners for the strike, the city's clergy also agreed with the proposed wage cut to end the strike. The New Bedford Ministerial Union sent a statement to the Textile Council and to the city's newspapers saying, "In view of the ever-increasing suffering and demoralization of the entire community, the present terms of the settlement should be accepted by the operatives."[17] Rev F. Taylor Wiehl of the Citizens Relief Committee concurred: "I believe that it would be for the best interests of all concerned to accept the compromise proposal."[18] Reverend Linden White, who also had opposed the wage cut throughout the strike, said from his pulpit the day before the vote, "If the Carpenter of Nazareth were in New Bedford faced with the proposition of ending this strike now, I believe that He would vote yes not as a conclusion of the main issue but because it is good strategy."[19]

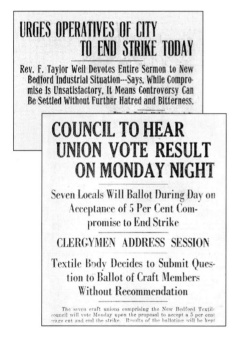

Clergy states its case. New Bedford's clergy strongly advocated that the Textile Council accept the five percent wage cut.
Ashley Scrapbook

The TMC, which had been excluded from the negotiations and whose members couldn't vote unless they also were members of the Council, pressed voters to reject the five percent wage cut. The TMC attacked the Council leaders for not rejecting "the sell out" in the strike committee, and asked mill workers to join their union in order to continue fighting.[20] Beal criticized the clergy in particular for supporting the compromise: "They can keep their damn mouths out of it. We can run our own business."[21]

"How Weavers Counted Their Strike Vote. Tellers at Work on Duff's Stage Hall." In the first ballot, the weavers union voted not to accept the mill owners' offer of a five percent wage cut. The turnout was very light; only about 20 percent of the weavers in the Textile Council voted.
Ashley Scrapbook

On Monday morning, October 1, the seven unions in the Council voted in their union halls on the five percent wage cut. Council leaders chose a weekday morning to limit the vote to striking members and to exclude members working at the tire plants and other mills that were still operating. Batty also asked Andrew Izyk, a member of the loomfixers union in the Council and treasurer of the TMC, to count the ballots for the loomfixers. Batty said that he "wanted to leave no uncertainty as to the counting of the ballots."[22]

With about two thousand mill workers voting, four of the seven craft unions, including the weavers and loomfixers, voted against the compromise, and by the rules of the Council the proposal was rejected.[23]

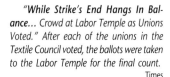

"While Strike's End Hangs In Balance... Crowd at Labor Temple as Unions Voted." After each of the unions in the Textile Council voted, the ballots were taken to the Labor Temple for the final count.
Times

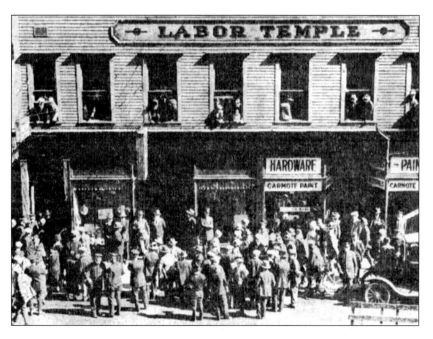

Our union never participated. The nearest we got to the negotiations was when the companies offered a return of five percent, and there was a referendum vote conducted by the other union. We told our people to go and vote against it, which they did, and it was defeated.

— Jack Rubenstein

When the tallies were announced, Council members inside the halls and jubilant TMC members waiting outside celebrated the results. The Council issued a statement rejecting the wage cut but kept the door open for further negotiations by adding that "the suggested settlement nowhere assured the workers that the same outrageous procedure would not occur again. Above and beyond the mere question of dollars and cents there is the human cry for consideration in matters as vital to workers as is one of wages."[24] Both the Council and the TMC prepared to carry on the strike. President McMahon of the UTW, who had favored the cost-cutting plan over the compromise wage cut, promised strike relief from the AFL to the Council.

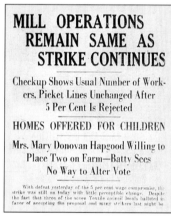

MILL OPERATIONS REMAIN SAME AS STRIKE CONTINUES

Checkup Shows Usual Number of Workers, Picket Lines Unchanged After 5 Per Cent Is Rejected

HOMES OFFERED FOR CHILDREN

Mrs. Mary Donovan Hapgood Willing to Place Two on Farm—Batty Sees No Way to Alter Vote

With defeat yesterday of the 5 per cent wage compromise, the strike was still on today with little perceptible change. Despite the fact that three of the seven Textile council locals balloted in favor of accepting the proposal and many strikers last night be

William Batty greets UTW President T.F. McMahon. McMahon had promised the strikers financial support and the union "access" to AFL organizations throughout the United States in return for their membership in the AFL.

Ashley Scrapbook

But the city's newspapers blamed the Council for continuing the strike by voting down the compromise. The editor of the *Evening Standard* wrote, "Thousands want to work, a very small number of strikers are keeping thousands of their fellows away from work. The workers have turned New Bedford against them. The workers have shown themselves selfish and indifferent to the needs of their fellow citizens."[25]

The newspapers called for another vote on the grounds that there had been some confusion about the time for voting. The newspapers had said that balloting would end at 5:00PM, but the craft unions started their meetings at 10:00AM and voted on the proposal, and most had finished counting the ballots by noon. A few days after the vote, the *Times* claimed that hundreds of Council members came to vote in the afternoon and found the balloting closed.[26] Batty countered, "Previous to the meetings, paid advertisements were inserted in the press announcing the hours at which each local would vote. Nothing was said about the privilege of balloting until 5:00PM."[27]

The newspapers weren't convinced. Holding the unions to a higher standard than he held for any city election, the *Times* editor wrote, "A single instance of illegal exclusion of a vote would discredit any regular election result. The same rule should apply in this voting which means so much to the entire city of New Bedford."[28]

An image of the future. *The newspapers had great hope for New Bedford. Having witnessed rapid growth in population and employment over the last forty years, and with harbor development plans in the works, many pundits saw the city as being on the threshold of becoming an important American center for commerce and industry. One key ingredient, emphasized in this* Times *illustration, was "The Spirit of We." Labor and capital would have to work together.*

Ashley Scrapbook

At first, Batty and the other Council leaders found little interest among their members for another vote.[29] But the newspapers and community leaders who had supported the Council leaders throughout the strike now pressured them to call for another vote. The *Times* editor wrote, "The regular textile unions in this city at the present time need and MUST HAVE REAL MEN at their heads if they are to survive."[30] When the Manufacturers' Association added to their offer a 30-day notice preceding any future wage cuts, the Council leaders gave in and called for a new vote on the five percent cut. This time they recommended that their members accept it.

On Saturday, October 6, five days after the first vote, Council members voted again on the mill owners' proposal. This time the police cordoned off each of the polling places, keeping the TMC away from the craft union meetings. Sergeant Velho arrested six TMC members for littering when they distributed hand bills urging the strikers to reject the five percent wage cut.[31]

MILL GATES QUIET AS FEW ADDITIONAL OPERATIVES ENTER

Riviere Slaps Rubenstein's Face In Argument Over Speed-up System—Pickets at Neild Chase Man

FUGITIVE HIDES IN ATTIC

Largest Number of Workers Reported at Nonquitt—Batty Joins Picket Line at Gosnold for Time

Quiet prevailed at all mill gates this morning as picket lines were reduced from 2,000 or so marchers of yesterday to 1,200 or 1,400 today, and crowds of spectators shrank from more than

CHIEF PUTS POLICE ON DUTY TO WATCH VOTING BY STRIKERS

100 Bluecoats Are Told to Keep Order as Locals Cast Ballots on 5 Per Cent Proposal

2,000 T. M. C. MEMBERS GATHER

Voice Protest Against Settlement, Then Leave Arena to Allow Union to Take Poll

Slashers' union members cast their votes.
Ashley Scrapbook

Police also arrested some TMC leaders to keep them away from the polling places.[32] Izyk wasn't allowed to count the loomfixers' ballots. James Simpson, leader of the carders union, whose members had cast the deciding vote against the compromise in the first ballot, announced that anyone belonging to the TMC would not be allowed to vote.[33]

> *In the meantime, quite a number of people were arrested. The TMC strike committee people were amongst them, including myself. After the strike was over, they released us. The manufacturers tried to create a conflict between the strikers and the people who came to help us from the outside. They said that they were agitators who were trying to destroy the country, and this had an effect. Don't forget, many of those workers were not American born. They were not American citizens, and it was a powerful thing to frighten them.*
> — Eula Mendes

With about the same number voting as before, all seven craft unions voted to accept the wage cut.

"TMC and Police Watch as Loomfixers vote. Police were sent to the Elm Rink to assure the UTW loomfixers a fair chance to vote on the peace plan there. The TMC had just finished a fight-to-the-death rally there and it was feared that there might be trouble."

Ashley Scrapbook

135

Returning to work at the Page Mill. On October 10, the day after the settlement, the mills reported operating at 50 percent capacity with 85 percent of their workforce on hand. "Everything was quiet at the noon hour and it seemed hard to believe that the mills had not been running normally all summer." The trolley line coming from Fall River was filled with migrant workers from New York and New Jersey, luggage in hand, who had arrived in Fall River looking for work, but had been directed to New Bedford.

Times

> *They had another vote, and our people boycotted it and of course it went though, which was probably a good thing even though at the time I opposed it. I don't know what happened, except maybe there was a feeling that this can't go on forever. There was a break in the sense that it represented a compromise, and eventually you can't strike forever.*
>
> — Jack Rubenstein

On Sunday, the day after the vote, the Manufacturers' Association announced it would reopen the mills on Monday. The mill owners called for weavers and loomfixers to return immediately but wouldn't say when the others could return to work. Everyone would have to apply and take their chances.

Seven thousand TMC supporters packed Saulnier's lot to hear Murdoch's promise to trade the police "blow for blow" on the picket lines

"Smiling Workers Rush to The Mills." Meanwhile the TMC continued to picket various mills. Many wore a yellow tag reading, "Strike against the wage cut, unite and help us to victory." At the Whitman Mill, when Officer Dufresne booked Bessie "Strawberry Shortcake" Katsikaris for striking a would-be worker in the back with a rock, "a threatening crowd surrounded him." Being alone and sensing danger, Dufresne "cooly walked away." He returned with "a small army of police and the neighborhood was cleaned out." Bessie escaped with help from the crowd but was arrested later.

Times

and keep the mills closed.[34] Police Chief McLeod called out his entire force for the expected confrontation.

The next morning the TMC failed to execute its promise to close the mills when thousands of mill workers entered the gates. The *Evening Standard* reported the mills were operating at almost full strength on the first day.[35] The TMC tried to prevent people from entering some mills in the South End, but the police quickly moved in and made dozens of arrests. Many mill workers on the picket lines tore off their TMC tags and slipped into the mills.[36]

The great New Bedford strike was over.

25 PLANTS RESUME WORK BY DECISION OF ASSOCIATION

Manufacturers Announce They Will Be Unable to Use Full Complement of Employes at Once

FIXERS AND WEAVERS WANTED

Mills to Increase Operations as Rapidly as Conditions Permit, They Assert —Confer on Merchandising

Augusto Pinto, TMC picket captain. "Jobs were closer to people than they are today because the main vein of their existence was getting each week's pay, each hour's pay. Their living was so closely connected with working. Back then there was no 'something else.' You work in the mill, and that mill was your life. That's the place you went to, that's the place you came back from, and there was very little in between because there wasn't enough income to take care of in between."
Standard-Times: Rubenstein

They have something to lose now.
In those days, they had nothing to lose.

– Jack Rubenstein

Bringing home some salvaged firewood along North Front Street, near Bennett and Grinnell Mill housing. [Jack Delano]

CHAPTER 8

THE AFTERMATH

The strike certainly helped to stimulate more interest in unionism. It made people aware of the need to band together, to have some sort of representation - some sort of power. They wanted the kind of power that would allow them to find out when cuts were going to come and when speed-ups were going to be installed. And the power to have the thing they wanted most of all - the right to a position, one the boss could not take away at will.

— Beatrice Pacheco

During the strike, the TMC had mobilized the mass of mill workers who long had been ignored by the Council. With tactics that its rivals could not imagine much less carry through, the TMC led thousands on the picket lines, at rallies and many other activities. About one thousand TMC members had been arrested during the strike, but they stoutly defended themselves on the picket lines and in the courts.

The Textile Council also led a successful strike. Although Council leaders compromised on the wage cut, they had forced the mill owners to negotiate with them, a great success for unions in the 1920s, and they remained the recognized voice of labor in the city. At the end of the long strike, the Council leaders retained the respect of the media and of political, business and professional groups. Their status protected their members from retaliation and gave them first chance at jobs.

But success proved the undoing of both unions. The TMC could not translate its organizing tactics during the strike into any long-term union organization, and the Council returned to its narrow focus on English skilled workers, ignoring the majority of New Bedford's mill workforce.

Ellen Dawson just before her release from jail. Ellen Dawson, 25 , was arrested on October 9 in a raid on TMC headquarters. While sitting on bench in the corridor, she was charged with being idle and disorderly. She had been arrested "so many times that I cannot count them." Dawson was sentenced to six months in jail and held on $500 surety.

Standard-Times

THE END OF THE TMC

During the strike the TMC leaders were recognized as legitimate though unwelcome union leaders, but after the strike, the police, newspapers, and other city establishments moved to drive them from the city. The day after the strike ended, the police arrested Dawson, Mendes, Murdoch, Keller, Rubenstein and 13 other TMC leaders for being idle and disorderly in what Chief Samuel McLeod described "as a sort of cleaning and sweeping up process."[1] Judge Frank Milliken sentenced each defendant to two to eight months in prison. Many TMC leaders left the city, never to return, when they were released on bail.

While the police were arresting TMC leaders, the mill owners were dispensing with TMC followers by refusing to hire them back.[2] During the strike, agents of the mill owners often took pictures of picket lines, and when they could, they spied on TMC meetings to identify members for blacklisting. When the mill workers returned to their jobs, the *Evening Standard* reported that "overseers of various departments stood at mill gates examining each worker. Here and there an undesirable was weeded out."[3]

The overseers cast their nets wide to catch anyone even suspected of union militancy. Some with little or no connection to the TMC got their jobs back a few months later, but TMC leaders who had worked in New Bedford's mills before the strike never were rehired and were forced to leave the city or work in other industries.[4]

The day the strike started, we were talking about the pickets that would be there, and I said, "Well, I won't go in past the pickets." Not because I wouldn't be a strikebreaker, but because I was afraid to go past them. There was a woman on the floor who was the head of the girls, and she must have

"The First Arrest in TMC South End Raid." On October 9, police moved "as elaborately as army maneuvers," sending squads to every mill. Motorcycle policeman acted as scouts; fast cars were kept running outside the substations, and police infiltrated TMC ranks the night before. At one mill where the crowd was boisterous, "the display of the new billies in the hands of police was sufficient to quiet them." The first eleven arrests took place at this food station on Potomska Street.

Times

told the boss what I said. As a result, he thought that I was influencing the other girls, and I didn't get my job back, not for a long, long time after the strike. I was just out of work.

Eventually a friend of my husband got me a job in the Dartmouth Mill. But I liked the other place better because it was cleaner. I went back to the Potomska, and again I asked for my old job back. They wouldn't give it to me. I asked why, and they told me it was because of what I had said. Just because of that! Then the boss said, "We don't want to hear anything about the unpleasantness of the strike. You can have your job back."

— Mary Greaves

I couldn't get a job in any of the other mills, so I went back to work for the Textile Mill Committees which continued even after the strike. We organized the various mills. We had what you call a union which was not really a union. Our union, our TMC was very poor. We had no money — the little bit that came in from dues after the strike was just for conducting whatever work that had to be conducted.

— Eula Mendes

The newspapers, which previously had supported civil rights for TMC leaders, applauded the police roundup and harassment. The *Times* called the TMC leaders "agents of destruction, who are hostile to the interests of every working man and woman and to the happiness and safety of their families."[5]

The *Evening Standard* warned that, "From here they will go elsewhere, to the scene of another labor fight where they will again pester unions and authorities alike. It is to be hoped that the government may get its case soon and that the threat of deportation may be of some effect upon radical activities in strikes."[6]

Young TMC members leave for the National Textile Workers Union (NTWU) founding convention in New York. At left is Elizabeth Donnelly, and Eula Mendes and Joe Figueiredo stand in the front row on the far right. TMC members Reid, Weisbord and Murdoch were elected president, secretary treasurer and 2nd vice president of the NTWU.

Ashley Scrapbook

Augusto Pinto. "We encouraged strikers to talk at our meetings because we were looking to develop leadership. Pinto never spoke at any of the meetings but give him a picket line sign or give him a picket, and he would do it night and day. He was very loyal to the fight."

Standard-Times: Rubenstein

Augusto Pinto had been arrested on the picket lines and convicted 22 times, but like 600 other TMC defendants he had appealed each count to superior court. In a special superior court session in March 1929, Pinto and the other TMC defendants were released by Superior Court Judge David Dillon, who said, "Such a disposition will end the recent industrial warfare so far as the court is concerned, invite industrial peace and encourage the repair of the damage already done to the defendants and to almost everyone else in New Bedford."[7]

Unfortunately for Pinto, the U.S. Immigration Service did not agree with Dillon and on October 23, 1931 forcibly placed him on a ship bound from Providence to Lisbon.[8] When he arrived in President Salazar's Portugal, a fascist dictatorship where militant labor leaders were not welcome, Pinto was sent to prison in Cape Verde and reportedly died en route, sending a shudder through New Bedford's Portuguese community.[9]

Although he didn't share Pinto's fate at the hands of a military dictator, William Murdoch was deported a month later to his native Scotland.

The TMC leaders were not faring very well outside of New Bedford either. Heady from their success in winning over the bulk of New Bedford's mill workers, the TMC leaders became the main organizers for the National Textile Workers Union (NTWU), the communist rival to the UTW. But they continued to focus on tactics rather than goals. In a series of strikes, mostly in the South, the new union brought thousands of people into picket lines but moved no closer to attaining its goals: decent wages and working conditions, a continuing organization representing workers and the eventual overthrow of capitalism.

The NTWU faced vicious opposition in the South. While leading a strike in Gastonia, North Carolina in 1929, Fred Beal was arrested for the murder of Sheriff O.F. Aderholt, who was killed in a shoot-out with the strikers. He and 15 others, including New Bedford veteran Amy Schechter, were charged with murder. When the prosecution brought a life-size dummy of the dead police chief into court, one of the jurors went mad, and Judge M.V. Barnhill declared a mistrial.

In the subsequent trial, Beal was found guilty of murder and sentenced to 17 to 20 years at hard labor. While on appeal, he jumped bail and escaped to the Soviet Union. But Beal was disappointed in life there and returned to the United States as a staunch anti-communist. Over the next few years, he wrote his autobiography, which ran as a serial in the Hearst papers. In January 1938, Beal was captured in Lawrence and returned to prison in North Carolina. Four years later, he was freed after an intense lobbying effort by the AFL and bitterly withdrew from the labor movement.[10]

In 1934, the NTWU, demoralized by its failure in the South, instructed its locals to join in with the UTW in its national strike and vanished soon after.

While the Textile Mill Committees had a good start, it was destroyed as a result of the fight within the Communist Party itself in '29 when the issue was not what's good for the textile workers or how to organize textile workers. The issue was whether you accepted communist directives from abroad or you didn't. And on that sort of rock any organization had to be destroyed, particularly when its roots had not sunk deeply into the community.

— Jack Rubenstein

The anti-communist hysteria after World War II finished the few remaining TMC leaders. Communist Party members and other political agitators were arrested under laws such as the McCarran-Walter Act, which provided 700 grounds for deporting aliens, including failure to register for fingerprinting within one month after their 14th birthday.[11]

On March 16, 1950, Eula Mendes, who at 18 had been secretary of the TMC, was arrested at her New Bedford home by the U.S. Immigration and Naturalization Service in a roundup of 39 people throughout the country and charged under the McCarran Act as a subversive alien. She had been born in Portugal, came here as a child and was never allowed to become a U.S. citizen. Front page headlines throughout New England in type usually reserved for declaration of war or peace proclaimed her arrest as a foreigner and a Communist. She was found guilty by an administrative law judge and sentenced to deportation.[12]

I had tried to get citizenship before, but when I applied for citizenship, they said, "You're a criminal, we can't give you citizenship." "Why?" "Because you have a crime record." "What do you mean I have a crime record?" "Well, you were arrested a number of times." I said, "Sure, during the strike," and he said, "That's against you as a criminal."

Later when the Second World War started, many foreign-born people were able to get into the army and eventually were able to get citizenship. Well, I decided I would try, but they said that they couldn't take foreign-born women.

Fred Beal at his murder trial in Gastonia. *When he returned to New Bedford after his conviction in North Carolina, Beal was asked by a policeman why he hung around with the foreigners. Beal replied, "When I was here with the foreigners, as the officer calls them, I got 6 months in jail, and while I was down South among one hundred percent American workers, I got 20 years."*

Standard-Times

Eula Mendes, at the time of her deportation; Augusto and Maria Pinto; and William Murdoch. *All except for Maria Pinto were deported after the strike.*

Standard-Times

143

Eula Mendes, known to her fellow workers as "Guandacio." Early in the strike, the *Times* wrote: "Miss Mendes appeared almost daily on the speaking platform, while her ready smile and sparkling brown eyes coupled with a conservativeness of expression have made her a favorite at the Potomska and Diman Street halls."

Standard-Times: Times

At the Wamsutta Mill, 1930s. Battery hand Irene Liberty fills the loom batteries with filled bobbins. For many weavers the number of looms that they operated doubled after the strike.

Standard-Times

When I asked why, they told me that I had to become a citizen first. I said, "but you take foreign-born men." "Well, that's different," they said, "because they are going to fight." And so there was no way of getting citizenship.

I was deported because I was not a citizen. Picking on foreign-born people was used during the McCarthy days as a pressure against people in general. Even though everybody thought I was an American citizen, my arrest had the effect of creating a lot of fear amongst a lot of the Portuguese people who were not citizens. Most of those people who were deported had to go to countries they had not seen, had not lived in, and most of them had been brought to the United States when they were children.

— Eula Mendes

Three years of legal appeals followed. She lost her last grounds for appeal when her husband, Joe Figueiredo, whom she had met during the strike, divorced her. In the spring of 1953, Mendes was taken to Ellis Island and scheduled for deportation to Salazar's Portugal, where Pinto's fate probably awaited her. She applied to several countries for asylum. When Poland accepted, her friends from New Bedford's Portuguese community raised the money for the flight, and on May 23, 1953, Mendes boarded a plane for Warsaw.

"When the plane took off from New York, I felt the Iron Curtain closing behind me," she wrote back to her friends in New Bedford.[13]

It's not easy to leave a country where you grew up, where your life was involved with so many friends and everything else. Then to go to a completely different country with a completely different language. And it wasn't easy for me to learn Polish. I still don't know Polish very well. And you have to start a completely new life.

— Eula Mendes

The Decline and Fall of the Textile Council

In keeping the mills closed for six months and then leading workers back into the mills despite TMC opposition, the Council soundly defeated the TMC, its rival union, and demonstrated to the mill owners that it had control over skilled labor. The Council survived the strike with its organization intact and retained its standing in the city's ruling establishment, a remarkable result in a period when labor unions were soundly defeated elsewhere.

Freed from the threat of the TMC, the craft unions in the Textile Council returned to their policy of excluding the bulk of New Bedford's mill workers. The Council leaders found comfort among their own and dropped their interest in recruiting workers other than English skilled workmen. The various fledging organizations for women, Portuguese and Polish workers quickly slipped from sight as the more militant Council labor organizers left town, never to be invited back by the Council leaders.

I think there is always the emergence of some people but I don't think the situation there under the Council's domination encouraged that too much. It was kind of a closed leadership.

— Frank Manning

Years later when I sat around talking with some people from the Textile Council, they were talking about the bloody foreigners, the bloody this and the bloody that. One fine day it dawned on me that they were talking about the French-Canadians who had probably been living in and around New Bedford for several generations. They were referring to them as bloody foreigners whereas these people themselves had not even acquired American citizenship 'cause the English didn't readily give up their citizenship.

— Jack Rubenstein

At the Gosnold Mill, 1930, Anna Bernado threads a shuttle. She was responsible for the operation of six looms, much below the demands of other mills following the strike. The Gosnold and the Hathaway mills began weaving rayon as well as cotton during the Depression years.
Spinner Collection

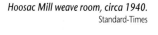

Hoosac Mill weave room, circa 1940.
Standard-Times

When New Bedford workers returned to the mills, many found their wages cut by more than the five percent they had accepted, and their work was speeded up.[14] Eventually, over the next few months, the mill owners installed most of the speedup contained in the Frieder Plan.[15]

We went back with what we thought was a ten percent cut. Once we got inside it was no ten percent cut, it was 20 percent, and in some crafts it was more than that. A weaver who was paid piece work would look at his pay and realize the size of the cut. When he went to complain, the boss would tell him, "Look, be quiet. If you don't want it, the next guy will take it." My wages in the spinning room were clipped 15 percent.

There was nothing we could do. We wouldn't have gotten to first base. Anyway, once we went back we were just individuals. After the strike there was no unity. You could have said to me, "Hey, Pete, I got a five dollar cut in my pay." I would have said, "Hey, you're lucky. I got a seven dollar cut."

— Pete Fauteux

I only had six looms for many, many years at the Pierce Mill. When I went to the Nashawena I was running twelve looms and Mr. Hayes, the overseer, came up to me and said, "How do you like your job, Alice?" I said, "Oh I think I'll be all right." My looms were running nice, and then he said, "But you know those twelve looms in the alley? They belong to you." I said, "You mean to tell me I have twenty-four looms?" Okay. That was Thursday and I figured I'd stick it out until Saturday because I might want a job back there someday.

On Friday a weaver came to me and said, "I got your job, Alice." She had told the boss that I was thinking of quitting. You know how things get around in those places. Saturday Mr. Hayes came in and said, "Come in Monday, Alice. I got a little job for you." Little umbrella cloth they had. It was about this wide, but I still had eighteen looms.

I liked my work. I always liked my work until we started getting more looms.

— Alice Green

Nashawena Mills weave room, 1929. The Nashawena had 5,835 looms, more than any other New Bedford mill. While most city mills were equipped with older looms, the Nashawena used the advanced Draper-Northrup automatic loom. This allowed the Nashawena to remain competitive while other New Bedford mills did not perform the change-over from their antiquated machinery.

Spinner Collection

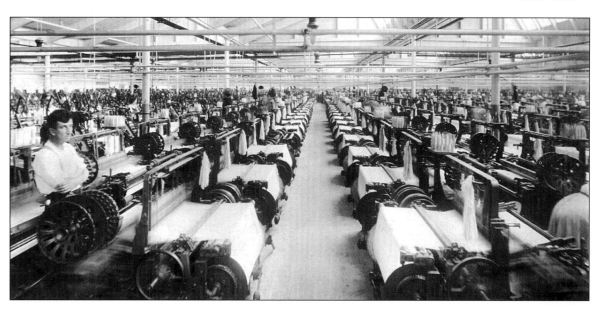

Fall River Scene, 1941. In Fall River, between 1925 and 1940, seventy-three textile mills shut down. The city was one of the first in the United States to declare bankruptcy during the Depression. The Massachusetts state legislature took over the city government and cut city services.
Jack Delano: Werly, Spinner II

Most textile workers did get their jobs back after the strike, and within a few months the mills employed almost as many people as they had before the strike. However, the Great Depression began in October 1929, almost exactly one year after the strike ended. By 1932, employment in the mills had been cut in half and wages had fallen by two-thirds. Textile workers who had lived close to the poverty level with jobs now slipped below it, and the increasing numbers without jobs were desperate.

Between 1929 and 1934, sixteen out of the 35 mills operating in the city permanently closed their gates. The Council leaders faced increasing pressure to accept lower wages and speedups. They resisted through careful plant-by-plant negotiations.[16] But economic conditions deteriorated further and textile workers throughout the country faced unemployment, starvation wages and a brutal work pace.

Strikers rally in school yard across from Goodyear Mill, 1934. In 1934, nearly one-half-million textile workers walked off their jobs across the country when the UTW declared a national textile strike. The union wanted to reduce the work week and keep the same weekly pay in order to employ more people. In New Bedford, 17,500 textile workers and two thousand garment workers joined the strike.
Standard-Times

William Batty leads pickets at the Goodyear Mill during the 1934 strike. The Textile Council concentrated their pickets at the Goodyear Mill, the only New Bedford mill that tried to operate during the strike. Once again the Council conducted a New Bedford kind of strike, "perfectly peaceful, perfectly good-humored." Thousands of people joined the picket lines, sang songs and exchanged "good natured banter with the police."
Standard-Times: Evening Standard

During the summer of 1934, Binns, as a member of the UTW's national executive council, chaired a committee investigating wages, hours and work-loads.[17] Binns's report, which recommended a 30-hour work week to reduce unemployment with no drop in weekly wages, set the stage for a national showdown with the mill owners. In August 1934, twenty representatives from New Bedford attended the special UTW convention in New York which declared a national textile strike to begin on September 1st. Binns was elected to the national strike committee.[18]

As in 1928, the Council completely shut down the cotton mills and kept them closed for the duration of the strike, even extending the strike to

Workers leaving the Goodyear Mill. On this day, September 5th, thousands of strikers picketed outside the Fiske and Goodyear awaiting the departure of those still working in the plants.
Standard-Times

"Children Enjoy the Textile Strike Excitement." Across the street from the Goodyear Mill, onlookers are contained by police as the Textile Council takes over picket duty. In contrast to the vicious battles on the picket lines throughout the rest of the country, no one crossed the picket line in New Bedford, and no one was arrested.
Standard-Times

the apparel shops which recently had opened in the city. Once again, as in 1928, the craft unions held large rallies in the city's parks, paid out strike benefits, opened soup kitchens and encouraged the clergy and civic leaders to support them. New Bedford remained a calm sea of solidarity surrounded by the stormy violence in the rest of the country. Hundreds of strikers in Rhode Island and elsewhere were seriously injured and some were killed on the picket lines in pitched battles with state militias, and thousands of strikers were arrested.[19] But New Bedford's mill owners did not challenge the picket lines, and no one was injured. The police did not make a single arrest in the city.[20]

Cheers at the Goodyear. After two days of mass picketing, the Goodyear owners said they would close their doors in order to safeguard workers from "the radical element who threaten them with violence." Here, along Ashley Park, workers are cheered as they leave the mill.
Standard-Times

Returning to work at the Nashawena Mill on the day after the strike settlement, 1934. Samuel Samuels, manager of the New Bedford Manufacturing Co., said, "While I have my personal feelings against regular employees who do not come to work this morning, I will not take them back to work under any consideration. I had warned them that if they did not come to work this morning they would lose their job."

Standard-Times

In the third week of the strike, President Roosevelt asked the UTW to call off the strike, and the union accommodated by declaring to mill workers across the country, "Your heroic strike ends in complete victory. Our triumph is one of the greatest in all labor history, and your officers salute you and congratulate you."[21] The Council went along with the settlement, but the Socialist party in New Bedford, led by veterans of the 1928 strike, was not fooled. The party called Roosevelt's request "meaningless and holding forth no hope to the textile workers" and "a deliberate strikebreaking appeal."[22]

Slashertender at Hathaway Mill, 1935. The National Recovery Act, passed in 1933, revived textile production in New Bedford because it set national standards that raised wages in the South. However, after the Supreme Court ruled the NRA unconstitutional, "the year 1935 marked the resumption of wholesale liquidation of New Bedford cotton textile mills."

Standard-Times: Wolfbein

The 1928 veterans were right. In New Bedford the Council still had the power to protect its members, but elsewhere mill owners used the strike settlement to eliminate thousands of labor leaders from their jobs, breaking the UTW.[23]

The depression in textiles worsened, and the Council succumbed to the pressure for wage cuts and work speedups in a losing effort to keep the mills open. In December, 1937, the Textile Council accepted a 12.5 percent pay cut.[24] In the same month, Batty proposed a plan to the 400 Neild Mill employees to put ten percent of their wages into a fund to pay the mill's creditors. A group of TMC veterans working in the mill opposed workers' paying the mill's debts, but Batty's plan easily passed. The mill workers paid, but the Neild Mill closed three months later.[25]

During the 1930s, 20 out of the 33 mills operating in the city permanently closed their gates.[26] At the start of the Depression, about 26,000 people worked in the mills; by 1938, only eight thousand remained.[27]

In May 1938, the Textile Council signed an agreement with the Cotton Manufacturers' Association which outlawed strikes and lockouts, established the 40-hour work week and recognized the Council as exclusive collective bargaining agents for all mill workers.[28] Batty called the pact, "our serious bid for industrial tranquility." In January 1941, the Council renewed the agreement for two years.[29]

When the agreement ran out, the Council faced its strongest and last challenge. In March 1943, the Textile Workers Organizers Committee (TWOC) of the Congress of Industrial Organizations (CIO) challenged the Council in a representation election under the Wagner Act of 1935. The TWOC was led by Antonio England, who had organized the city's rayon

Textile workers entering mill gates, 1941. In 1937, New Bedford's unemployment rate was 32 percent, the second highest of any city in the United States. In 1941, the U.S. Supreme Court approved the Fair Labor Standards Act, reducing the wage differences between the North and the South. "It is the best piece of news that I've seen in a long time," said Textile Council President, William Baron.

Jack Delano: Wolfbein

Mariano Bishop, Antonio England and William Batty. Born in Sao Miguel in the Azores, Bishop began working in Fall River's mills when he was ten. As the business agent for the UTW, he led the 1934 strike in Fall River and during the 1940s organized most of New England's textile mills into the Textile Worker Union of America. In 1952, the year before he died, Bishop was elected executive vice president of the TWUA, a national union with over 300,000 members. The statue of him in the Flint section of Fall River is one of the few monuments to a labor leader in the United States.
Standard-Times: Kelly

workers in 1932, and Mariano Bishop from Fall River. During the 1930s, the CIO built widespread working-class unity and won union bargaining rights for millions of U.S. workers by forming strong national unions in steel, autos and other industries. Frank Manning, Donald Thompson and other militant Textile Council organizers from the 1928 strike joined with TMC veterans to support the CIO's challenge to the Council.

We felt that the Textile Council ought to be interested in better labor legislation. We also felt that they should be interested in old age pensions, unemployment insurance, minimum wage none of which were in effect in those days. That's part of what education is about. We felt that the Textile Council did a good job according to the way they'd been brought up and according to the way that they'd been doing things, but they were not really advocates for the workers in the larger sense, and they should be.

— Rev. Donald Thompson

Scrapping looms from Wamsutta Mills, 1958. The Wamsutta was purchased by M. Lowenstein & Sons in 1954, at a time when the mill was running at full capacity. The company, which operated a number of mills in the South, was one of the largest textile organizations in the United States. In 1958, Lowenstein closed the mill that had started New Bedford's industry but kept the Wamsutta name. Today, Wamsutta cottons are made in South Carolina.

Standard-Times

When you have a large number of people involved, amazing things happen. People that you've never even looked at twice suddenly become leaders. Ideas come from those obscure, and least expected, and so forth. That is why I've always been very careful not to close my ears to anybody. You know, wisdom is not confined to any one group.

It was very inspirational to work for the CIO. It really put a light on the laborer. It's really nice to know that we were reaching out to the unskilled and semiskilled and raising them up on the economic ladder.

— Frank Manning

On March 31, 1943, the CIO won election in ten mills by 300 votes out of ten thousand ballots, while the Council won representation only in the Hoosac Mill. For the first time in his long career, Batty, who would soon take a government job on the War Labor Board, was silent. The Council continued for a few years as a small union representing only a few hundred workers at the Hoosac Mill.

Although he had not worked in the mills in 1928, England spoke for two generations of mill workers who long had been excluded from the Textile Council: "Today is the fulfillment of our promise to the people of New Bedford to give the workers a chance to vote, an opportunity denied them for years. The workers are now in full possession of their democratic rights — rights which many of them never had, even within their own unions."[30]

Textile mill working all night, 1941.
Not until the mid-1930s did New Bedford's mills work throughout the night. This move was prompted by marketing organizations and selling houses concerned with diminishing commissions, and "whose primary consideration is volume and not quality."
Jack Delano: Wolfbein

BIBLIOGRAPHY

INTERVIEWS

Alves, Mary. By D. Bastarache. New Bedford MA. 8/31/81.
Andre, Manuel. By B. Pacheco. New Bedford MA. 10/6/80.
Araujo, Hilda. By R. Aaronson. New Bedford MA.
Batty, Harry J. By D. Georgianna. New Bedford MA. 6/18/84.
Buhle, Paul. By R. Aaronson. Providence RI. 5/31/84.
Cabral, Mr. & Mrs. Joaquim. By D Bastarache. New Bedford MA. 4/29/81.
Correira, Angie & Ray Combra. By D. Georgianna. New Bedford MA.
Correira, Angie. By D. Bastarache. New Bedford MA.
Crook, Margaret. By D. Bastarache. New Bedford MA.
DeGrasse, Quinton. By J. Anderson & J. Thomas, New Bedford MA. 3/81.
DeRoches, Mary. By D. Bastarache. New Bedford MA. 4/30/81.
Duff, Beatrice. By R. Aaronson. New Bedford MA. 5/4/84.
Duprey, Nora. By D. Georgianna & T. Stone. Lakeville MA. 12/1/81.
Edwards, Mary. By R. Aaronson. New Bedford MA.
Fauteux, Pete. By D. Bastarache. Fairhaven MA. 1/14/81.
Fauteux, Pete. By D. Bastarache & D. Georgianna. Fairhaven MA. 1/29/81.
Fernandes, Manuel. By B. Pacheco. New Bedford MA.
Greaves, Mary & Charles. By D. Georgianna. New Bedford MA. 12/3/80.
Green, Alice & John. By D. Georgianna. Fairhaven MA. 7/21/81.
Green, Alice. By D. Bastarache. New Bedford MA.
Howcroft, Gladys. By D. Bastarache. New Bedford MA.
Irwin, Marguerite. By D. Bastarache. New Bedford MA.
Isherwood, William. By M. Butler. No. Dartmouth MA. 1/23/80.
Law, Mary. By G. Schultz. New Bedford MA. 5/7/80.
Lebeau, Oliva. By D. Georgianna. New Bedford MA. 11/25/80.
Levesque, Joseph. By D. Bastarache & D. Georgianna. New Bedford MA.
Manning, Frank. By D. King. Boston MA.
Manning, Frank. By R. Aaronson. Boston MA. 8/8&18/81.
Marginson, Agnes & Victor. By D. Georgianna. New Bedford MA. 12/10/80.
Meggison, Robert. By S. Schinas. New Bedford MA. 11/21/80.
Mello, William. By D. Georgianna. New Bedford MA. 12/7/80.
Milotte, Isabelle Batty. By L. Beatrice. New Bedford MA.
Nardella, Luigi. By R. Aaronson. Cranston RI. 10/10/81.
O'Connor, Harvey. By I. Costa & D. Georgianna. Little Compton RI.
Oliver, Arnold. By D. Bastarache. New Bedford MA. 6/11/81.
Pacheco, Beatrice. By R. Aaronson. New Bedford MA. 10/8/80.
Papandreu, Eula Mendes. By D. Georgianna. Warsaw, Poland. 8/1-4/85.
Papandreu, Eula Mendes. By R. Reeve & J. Stauder. Warsaw, Poland. 7/2&3/87.
Perry, Arthur. By D. Bastarache. New Bedford MA. 11/18/81.
Potvin, Rosario. By B. Pacheco. New Bedford MA. 10/6/80.
Ramos Joseph. By M. DeCicco & J. Thomas. New Bedford MA. 3/81.
Reagan, John. By S. Schinas. New Bedford MA. 10/10/80.
Ripley, George. By B. Pacheco. New Bedford MA. 12/13/80.
Roderigues, Mary. By D. Bastarache. New Bedford MA. 4/8/81.
Rubenstein, Jack. By D. Georgianna. Dumont NJ. 9/2/80.
Rubenstein, Jack. By G. Schultz. New York NY. 8/19/80.
Saulnier, Al. By I. Costa & D. Georgianna. New Bedford MA. 8/25/81.
Severs, Alfred. By R. Aaronson. No. Dartmouth MA. 10/28/81.
Shaer, Sam. By R. Aaronson. No. Dartmouth MA. 8/2/81.
Silveira, Carrie. By D. Georgianna & R. Aaronson. New Bedford MA.
Souza, Anthony. By D. Georgianna. No. Dartmouth MA. 3/2/92
Thompson, Reverend Donald. By D. King. Boston MA.
Thompson, Reverend Donald. By R. Aaronson. Boston MA. 8/8&18/81
Watson, Fred. By G. Schultz. New Bedford MA. 12/14/80.

NEWSPAPERS

Boston Globe. Boston MA. 1950.
Daily Herald. Fall River MA. 1928.
Daily Worker. New York NY. 1928.
Evening Standard. New Bedford MA. 1897-1932.
Federated Press. Chicago. IL. 1928.
Morning Mercury. New Bedford MA. 1897, 1898, 1912, 1928.
New Bedford Times. New Bedford MA. 1922, 1928, 1929.
Standard-Times. New Bedford MA. 1941, 1942, 1950, 1953.

PUBLISHED SOURCES

Adamic, Louis. 1934. *Dynamite: The Story of Class Violence in America*. New York: Viking Press.
Allen, Everett S. 1973. *Children of the Light: The Rise and Fall of New Bedford Whaling and the Death of the Arctic Fleet*. Boston: Little, Brown & Co.
Asher, Martha Stone. 1990. "Recollections of the Passaic Textile Strike of 1926." *Labor's Heritage*. 2 2: 4-23.
Beal, Fred. 1937. *Proletarian Journey: New England, Gastonia, Moscow*. New York: Hillman, Curl Inc.
Belfrage, Cedric. 1989. *The American Inquisition 1945-1950*. New York: Thunder Mouth's Press.
Bedford, Henry F. 1966. *Socialism and the Workers in Massachusetts*. Amherst: University of Massachusetts Press.
Bernstein, Irving. 1972. *The Lean Years: a History of the American Worker. 1920-1933*. Boston: Houghton Mifflin Company.
Bimba, Anthony. 1927. *History of the American Working Class*. Reprint. New York: Greenwood Press.
Boss, Judith A. and Joseph D. Thomas. 1983. *New Bedford: A Pictorial History*. Norfolk: Donning Company Publishers.
Blanchard, Paul. 1928. "New Bedford Goes on Strike." *The New Republic*. 5/23.
Brecher, Jeremy. 1972. *Strike!* New York: Straight Arrow Books.
Brody, David. 1987. *Labor in Crisis: The Steel Strike of 1919*. Urbana: University of Illinois Press.
Buhle, Mary Jo, Paul Buhle and Dan Georgakas. 1990. *Encyclopedia of the American Left*. New York: Garland Books.
Buhle, Paul. 1987. *Marxism in the USA: From 1870 to the Present Day*. London: Verso.
Burgy, J. Herbert. 1932. *The New England Cotton Textile Industry: A Study in Industrial Geography*. Baltimore: Waverly Press.
Cahn, William. 1980. *Lawrence 1912 : The Bread and Roses Strike*. New York: Pilgrim Press.
Cameron, Ardis. 1985. "Bread and Roses Revisited: Women's Culture and Working-Class Activism in the Lawrence Strike of 1912." *Women's Work and Protest: A Century of U.S. Women's Labor History*. New York: Routledge and Kegan Paul.
Coolidge, John. 1942. *Mill and Mansion*. New York: Columbia University Press.
Copeland, Melvin Thomas. 1912. *The Cotton Manufacturing Industry of the United States*. Cambridge: Harvard University Press.
Davis, Lance, Robert Gallman and Theresa Hutchins. 1988. "The Decline of U.S. Whaling: Was the Stock of Whales Running Out?" *Harvard Business History Review*. 62:569-595.
Dickens, Charles. 1842. *American Notes and Pictures from Italy*. Reprint. London: Oxford University Press.
Dunn, Robert and Jack Hardy. 1931. *Labor and Textiles*. New York: International Publishing.
Dunwell, Steve. 1978. *The Run of the Mill*. Boston: David R. Godine.

Ely, Richard. 1905. *Labor Movement in America.* New York: Macmillan.

Foner, Philip. 1979. *Women and the American Labor Movement.* New York: Free Press.

Gerstle, Gary. 1989. *Working Class Americanism: The Politics of Labor in a Textile City, 1914-1960.* New York: Cambridge University Press.

Green, James. 1980. *The World of the Worker: Labor in Twentieth Century America.* New York: Farrar, Straus and Giroux.

Gutman, Herbert. 1977. *Work, Culture and Society in Industrializing America.* New York: Random House.

Hall, J., J. Leloudis, R. Korstad, M. Murphy, L.A. Jones and C.D. Daly. 1987. *Like a Family: The Making of a Southern Cotton World.* Chapel Hill: University of North Carolina Press.

Hohman, Elmo. 1928. *The American Whaleman: a Study of Life and Labor in the Whaling Industry.* New York: Longmans, Green and Co.

Hough, Henry Beetle. 1946. *Wamsutta of New Bedford 1846-1946: A Story of New England Enterprise.* New Bedford: Wamsutta Mills.

Kelly, Richard. 1956. *Nine Lives for Labor.* New York: F.A. Praeger.

Kugler, Richard. 1975. *New Bedford and Old Dartmouth: A Portrait of a Region's Past.* New Bedford: Old Dartmouth Historical Society.

Lahne, Herbert J. 1944. *The Cotton Mill Worker.* New York: Farrar & Rinehart.

Lauck, W. Jett. 1919. "The Cotton-Mill Operatives of New England." *Atlantic Monthly.*

Lenin, V. I. 1967. "Left-Wing Communism - An Infantile Disorder." *Selected Works of V. I. Lenin.* New York: International Publishing.

Lovett, Robert Morss. 1928. "New Bedford's Strike - A Knockout or a Comeback?" *The New Republic,* 9/12.

McMullin, Thomas. 1982. "Lost Alternative: The Urban Industrial Utopia of William D. Howland." *New England Quarterly.*

Montgomery, David. 1967. *Beyond Equality: Labor and the Radical Republicans, 1862-1972.* Reprint. Urbana: University of Illinois Press.

Montgomery, David. 1987. *The Fall of the House of Labor.* Cambridge: Cambridge University Press.

Monthly Labor Review. "1928. Wages and Hours of Labor in Cotton-Goods Manufacturing."

Morison, Samuel Eliot. 1921. *The Maritime History of Massachusetts. 1783-1860.* Reprint. Boston: Northeastern University Press.

Nadir, Moshe. 1931. *On Vacation.* Translated from Yiddish by Andrea Kurtzman. New York: Frieheit Press.

Nearing, Scott. 1972. *The Making of a Radical.* New York: Harper & Row.

Pease, Zephaniah W. 1918. *History of New Bedford.* New York: Lewis Historical Publishing Co.

Pease, Zephaniah W. 1907. *100th Anniversary of the New Bedford Mercury.* New Bedford.

Perlman, Selig and Phillip Taft. 1935. "History of Labor in the United States, 1896-1932, Vol IV." *Labor Movements.* New York: MacMillan.

Robinson, Harriet Hanson. 1898. *Loom and Spindle.* Reprint. Kailua: Press Pacifica.

Santos, Michael W. 1985. "Community and Communism: The 1928 New Bedford Textile Strike." *Labor History,* 26:230-249

Saposs, David. 1926. *Left Wing Unionism.* New York: International Publishing.

Symons, Julian. 1957. *The General Strike a Historical Portrait.* London: Cresset Press.

Thomas, Edmund B. Jr. 1987. "The New England Textile Strike of 1922: Focus on Fitchburg." *Historical Journal of Massachusetts.* 15 1: 21-32.

Thomas, Joseph D. 1980. *Spinner: People and Culture in Southeastern Massachu-setts, Vol. I.* New Bedford: Spinner Publications.

——. 1981. *Spinner: People and Culture in Southeastern Massachusetts, Vol. II.* New Bedford: Spinner Publications.

——. 1984. *Spinner: People and Culture in Southeastern Massachusetts, Vol. III.* New Bedford: Spinner Publications.

——. 1986. *Spinner: People and Culture in Southeastern Massachusetts, Vol. IV.* New Bedford: Spinner Publications.

Walton, Perry. 1925. *The Story of Textiles.* New York: Tudor Publishing Co.

Ware, Caroline. 1931. *The Early Cotton Manufacture.* New York: Hart, Schaffner & Marx.

Ware, Norman. 1924. *The Industrial Worker: 1840-1860.* Chicago: Quadrangle Books. Reprint. Houghton Mifflin Co.

Weisbord, Albert. 1926. *Passaic: The Story of a Struggle Against Starvation Wages and for the Right to Organize.* Reprint. New York: AMS.

Weisbord, Albert. 1937. *The Conquest of Power: Liberalism, Anarchism, Syndicalism, Socialism, Fascism and Communism.* New York: Covici-Friede.

Weisbord, Vera Buch. 1977. *A Radical Life.* Bloomington: Indiana University Press.

William Whitman Company, Inc. 1921. *Wool and Cotton in All Forms from Yarn to Fabric.* New York.

Williams, Jerry. 1982. *And Yet They Come: Portuguese Immigration from the Azores to the United States.* Staten Island: Center for Migration Studies.

Wolfbein, Seymour. 1944. *The Decline of a Cotton Textile City: A Study of New Bedford.* New York: Columbia University Press.

Young, Thomas M. 1902. *The American Cotton Industry: A Study of Work and Workers.* London: Methuen.

UNPUBLISHED SOURCES

Ashley, Mayor Charles S. Scrapbook. 1892-1936. New Bedford Public Library.

Boston Chamber of Commerce. 1926. "The Cotton Manufacturing Industry of New England."

Boyce, Larry. 1984. "The Financial Condition of New Bedford's Cotton Textile Industry During the 1920s." mimeo.

Brooks, Robert. 1935. "The United Textile Workers of America." Ph.D. diss., Yale University .

Crapo, Henry Howland. 1937. "The Story of Cotton and Its Manufacture into Cloth in New Bedford." New Bedford: Old Dartmouth Historical Sketches, No. 67.

Dawley, Alan. 1986. "Authority and Insubordination: The United States in the Great War." mimeo.

Georgianna, Daniel. 1984. "The Textile Industry in New England During the 1920s." mimeo.

Isherwood, William. 1981. "New Bedford's Textile Era." mimeo.

Katz, Jamie W. 1974. "Opportunity, Exclusion, and the Immigrant: Textile Workers in New Bedford, Massachusetts, 1890-1930." honors thesis. Harvard University.

Langshaw, Walter. 1939. "Press Clippings Pertaining to the Efforts and Achievements of Walter Langshaw." New Bedford Free Public Library.

McCartin, Joseph. 1990. "The Textile Workers' Great War: the Rhode Island Loomfixers' Strike of 1918 and the Failure of Wartime Organizing." mimeo.

McDevitt, Joseph I. 1978. "The House of Rotch: Whaling Merchants of Massachusetts, 1734-1828." Ph.D. diss., American University.

McKenna, James F. "New Bedford Textile Strike of 1928." Federal Writers Project Assignment.

McMullin, Thomas. 1976. "Industrialization and Social Change in a Nineteenth-Century Port City: New Bedford, Massachusetts, 1865-1900." Ph.D. diss., University of Wisconsin.

Murphy, Teresa Anne. 1982. "Labor, Religion and Moral Reform in Fall River, Massachusetts, 1800-1845." Ph.D diss., Yale University.

Office of Historic Preservation. 1977. "New Bedford Mills." New Bedford.

Schultz, Gale. 1980. "The G-Loom Years." mimeo.

Silvia, Philip T. Jr. 1973. "The Spindle City: Labor, Politics, and Religion in Fall River." Ph.D diss., Fordham University.

Stone, Patricia, M. 1982. "The New Bedford Textile Workers' Strike of 1928: An Unresolved Conflict." Honors thesis, Brown University.

Sweetser, General E. Leroy. 1923. "Report of a Special Investigation into Conditions in the Textile Industry in Massachusetts and the Southern States." Massachusetts Department of Labor and Industries.

Whitney, Jessamine S. 1920. "Infant Mortality: Results of a Field Study in New Bedford, Massachusetts, Based on Births in One Year." U.S. Department of Labor, Children's Bureau.

FOOTNOTES

CHAPTER I

1. McMullin, "Industrialization and Social Change," p. 5.
2. Hohman, *The American Whaleman*, p. 9.
3. McMullin, op. cit., p. 6.
4. Morison, *The Maritime History of Massachusetts*, pp. 319-321.
5. McMullin, op. cit., p. 6; Allen, *Children of the Light*, p. 82.
6. McMullin, op. cit., p. 12.
7. Davis, et al, *The Decline of U.S. Whaling*, p. 572.
8. Allen, op. cit., p. 222.
9. McMullin, op. cit., p. 13.
10. Ware, Caroline, *The Early New England Cotton Manufacture*, p. 30.
11. Ibid., p.145; Coolidge *Mill and Mansion.*, pp. 15-16.
12. Ware, op. cit., p. 63.
13. Coolidge, op. cit., p. 12.
14. Coolidge, op. cit., pp. 20-21.
15. Dickens, *American Notes,* pp. 66-70.
16. Michel Chevalier quoted in Ware, op. cit., p. 202.
17. Ibid., p. 238.
18. Ibid., p. 241.
19. Robinson, *Loom and Spindle*, p. 47.
20. Ibid., p. 43.
21. Ware, op. cit., p. 269.
22. Ibid., p. 274.
23. Ibid., p. 275 ; Robinson, op. cit., pp. 51-52.
24. Ware, op. cit., p. 215.
25. Ibid., pp. 230-235.
26. Ibid., p. 109.
27. Copeland, *The Cotton Manufacturing Industry,* p. 27.
28. Hall, et al, *Like a Family*, p 46; Wolfbein, *The Decline of A Cotton Textile City*, pp. 68-73.
29. Ware, op. cit., pp. 107-108.
30. McMullin, op. cit., p. 6.
31. Ibid., p. 15; Hough, *Wamsutta of New Bedford*, p. 15.
32. Ibid., pp. 11-12.
33. Ibid., p. 27.
34. Ibid., pp. 32-40; Letter from W.W. Crapo to Ridley Watts, Old Dartmouth Historical Society.
35. Wolfbein, op. cit., p. 155.
36. Ibid., p. 156; McMullin, op. cit., p. 23.
37. Ibid., p. 30.
38. Ibid., p. 34.
39. Ibid., pp. 35-40.
40. Ibid., p. 66.
41. Ibid., p. 10.
42. Ibid., pp. 50-55.
43. Ibid., pp. 41-43.
44. Ibid., p. 43.
45. McMullin, "Lost Alternatives," p. 43.
46. McMullin, "Industrialization and Social Change," pp. 221, 248.
47. Katz, "Opportunity, Exclusion, and the Immigrant," pp. 26, 27.
48. McMullin, op. cit., pp. 43-45.
49. Lahne, *The Cotton Mill Worker*, p. 104; Whitney, "Infant Mortality," p. 41.
50. Lahne, op. cit., p. 106.
51. Whitney, op. cit., pp. 37-39.
52. Ibid., pp. 22-25.

CHAPTER II

1. Montgomery, *Beyond Equality*, p. 165.
2. Murphy, "Labor, Religion and Moral Reform," pp. 128-130.
3. Montgomery, op. cit., p. 277.
4. Ibid., pp. 282-290; McMullin, op. cit., pp, 208-213, has a slightly different story.
5. Ibid., pp. 217-221.
6. Ibid., p. 216.
7. Ibid., p. 220.
8. Ibid., p. 227.
9. Ibid., p. 228.
10. Ibid., p. 223.
11. Silvia, "The Spindle City," pp. 540-543.
12. McMullin, op. cit., p. 241.
13. Boston *Sunday Post*, 1/16/98.
14. Boston *Herald.*, 2/5/98.
15. McMullin, op. cit., p. 239.
16. *Evening Standard*, 2/10/98.
17. McMullin, op. cit., p. 247.
18. *Evening Standard*, 4/15/98, p. 4.
19. Ibid., 1/20/98.
20. McMullin, op. cit., p. 242.
21. Ibid., p. 244.
22. *Evening Standard,* 2/10/98.
23. Ibid., 2/12/98
24. *Morning Mercury*, 3/11/98, p. 5.
25. Ibid., 4/5/98, p. 5.
26. Ibid., 4/5/98, p. 1.
27. *Evening Standard*, 4/11/98, p. 2.
28. McMullin, op. cit., p. 245.
29. Katz, op. cit., p. 76.
30. McMullin, op. cit., p. 244; Katz, op. cit., p. 53.
31. Ibid., p. 53; *Evening Standard*, 4/17/98, p. 9.
32. Katz, op. cit., p. 55.
33. Ibid., p. 54.
34. Ibid., p. 54.
35. Ibid., pp. 60-64; Saposs, *Left Wing Unionism*, p. 98.
36. Lahne, op. cit., p. 195.
37. Ibid., p. 201; Katz, op. cit., p. 62.
38. Wolfbein, op. cit.,, pp. 84-86.
39. Ibid., pp. 10, 157.
40. Ibid., p. 156, 158.
41. Katz, op. cit., p. 65.
42. Ashley,. "Scrapbook," April, 1920, p. 122.
43. Wolfbein, op. cit., p. 159.
44. Lahne, op. cit., p. 209.

CHAPTER III

1. *Evening Standard*, 4/9/28, pp. 1, 3.
2. Ibid., 4/20/28, p. 6.
3. Ibid., 4/9/28, p. 2.
4. Ashley,. op. cit., April, 1928, p. 72.
5. *Evening Standard*, 4/9/28, p. 3.
6. Ibid., 4/18/28, p. 7.
7. Silvia, op. cit., pp. 711-712.
8. *Evening Standard*, 1/26/28, p. 9.
9. Boyce, "The Financial Condition," pp. 3-10.
10. *Evening Standard*, 4/11/28, p. 2.
11. McKenna, "Federal Writers' Project," p. 4.
12. *Evening Standard*, 4/13/28, p. 2.
13. Ashley, op. cit.,. April, 1928, p. 64.
14. *Evening Standard*, 4/16/28, p. 2.
15. Ibid, 4/17/28, p. 3
16. *Times*, 4/17/28, p. 1.

CHAPTER IV

1. *Evening Standard*, 4/24/28, p. 8.
2. Ibid., 4/25/28, p. 2.
3. Ashley, op. cit., April, 1928, p. 124.
4. *Evening Standard*, 4/24/28, p. 7.
5. Ashley, op. cit., April, 1928, p. 153.
6. *Evening Standard*, 5/4/28, p. 2.
7. Ashley, op. cit., April, 1928, p. 127.
8. *Times* , 4/18/28, p. 4.
9. *Times* , 4/18/28, p. 4.
10. *Evening Standard*, 6/16/28, p. 3.
11. *Evening Standard*, 9/4/28, p. 2; 8/19/28, p. 21.
12. *Evening Standard*, 6/3/28, p. 3.
13. Ibid., 9/19/28, p. 21.
14. Times, 6/15/28, p. 2.
15. *Evening Standard,*, 10/12/28, p. 1.
16. Lahne, op. cit., p. 212; *Evening Standard*, 5/7/28, p. 1.
17. Santos, "Community and communism," p. 233.
18. Langshaw, "Press Clippings," p. 364.
19. Blanchard, "New Bedford goes on Strike," p. 10.
20. Ashley, op. cit., April, 1928, p. 113.
21. Ashley, op. cit., April, 1928, p. 120.
22. *Evening Standard*, 5/9/28, p. 6.
23. McMullin, op. cit., pp. 183-188.
24. *Evening Standard*, 4/16/28, p. 4.
25. Ibid., 5/14/28, p. 1.
26. Ibid., 4/24/28, p. 7.
27. Ibid., 5/10/28, p. 1.
28. Ibid., 2/16/29, p. 2.
29. Ibid., 4/13/28, p. 1.
30. Ibid., 4/16/28, p. 2.
31. Ibid., 5/15/28, p. 1.
32. Langshaw, op. cit., p. 366.
33. Langshaw, op. cit., p. 375.

CHAPTER V

1. Asher, "Recollections of the Passaic Textile Strike," p. 11.
2. Ibid., p. 22; Bimba, *History of the American Working Class* , has a different version of result. pp. 309-310.
3. Ibid., pp. 343-344.
4. Beal, *Proletarian Journey,* p. 98.
5. Ibid., p. 99; Ashley, op. cit., April, 1928, p. 64.
6. *Evening Standard,* 7/22/28, p. 2.
7. Beal op. cit., p. 99; Papandreu interview.
8. *Morning Mercury,* 4/19/28, p. 14.
9. *Evening Standard,* 5/25/28, p. 2; Rubenstein interview.
10. *Evening Standard,* 5/1/28, p. 13.
11. Ibid., 5/5/28, p. 1.
12. Ibid., 5/6/28, p. 2.
13. Ibid., 5/3/28, p. 6.
14. Ibid., 4/18/28, p. 1.
15. Ibid., 5/6/28, p. 2.
16. Times, 5/7/28, p. 1.
17. *Evening Standard,* 5/29/28, p. 2.
18. Ibid., 4/18/28, p. 2.
19. Ibid., 4/18/28, p. 2.
20. Ibid., 5/1/28, p. 2.
21. Ibid., 5/5/28, p. 1; 5/10/28, p. 1; 5/14/28, p. 1.
22. Ibid., 5/22/28, p. 1.
23. Burgy, *The New England Cotton Textile Industry,* p. 170.
24. *Evening Standard,* 6/12/28, p. 18.
25. Ibid., 6/12/28, p. 18.
26. Ibid., 7/3/28, p. 7.
27. Ibid., 5/9/28, p. 2.
28. Ibid., 5/24/28, p. 5.
29. Ibid., 6/4/28, p. 1.
30. Ibid., 5/21/28, p. 1.
31. Ibid., 5/16/28, p. 3.
32. Fauteux interview.
33. *Evening Standard,* 6/22/28, p. 2.
34. Ibid., 6/16/28, p. 3.

CHAPTER VI

1. *Evening Standard,* 4/17/28, p. 1; 5/1/28, p. 1; 5/6/28, p. 2.
2. Ibid., 5/8/28, p. 1.
3. *Times* , 5/10/28, p. 2.
4. *Evening Standard,,* 6/26/28, p. 1.
5. Ibid., 6/25/28, p. 1.
6. Ibid., 6/14/28, p. 1.
7. Ibid., 6/14/28, p. 9.
8. Ibid., 6/25/28, p. 13.
9. Ibid., 6/20/28, p. 2.
10. Ibid., 6/22/28, p. 2.
11. Ibid., 6/22/28, p. 2.
12. *Times,* 6/21/28, p. 1.

13. *Evening Standard,* 6/28/28, p. 15.
14. Ibid., 7/1/28, p. 1., 7/13/28, p. 1.
15. Ibid., 7/2/28, p. 2.
16. Ibid., 7/13/28, p. 1.
17. Ibid., 6/27/28, p. 1.
18. *Times,* 7/7/28, p. 2.
19. *Evening Standard,* 7/9/28, p. 1; *Times,* 7/9/28, p. 1.
20. *Evening Standard,* 7/7/28, p. 2.
21. Ibid., 7/15/28, p. 2.
22. Ibid., 7/17/28, p. 2.
23. *Morning Mercury,* 7/18/28, p. 14.
24. *Evening Standard,* 7/17/28, p. 2.
25. *Times,* 7/16/28, p. 1.
26. *Evening Standard,* 7/18/28, p. 4.
27. Ibid., 7/18/28, p. 4.
28. Ibid., 7/20/28, p. 1.
29. Ibid., 7/19/28, p. 2.
30. Ibid., 6/1/28, p. 1.
31. Ibid., 7/23/28, p. 1
32. Ashley, op. cit., July, 1928, p. 167.
33. *Evening Standard,* 7/25/28, p. 1.
34. Ibid., 7/25/28, p. 1.
35. Lovett, "New Bedford's Strike," p. 91.
36. *Evening Standard,* 8/7/28, p. 4.
37. Ibid., 8/15/28, p. 2.
38. Ibid., 8/15/28, p. 6.
39. Ibid., 6/29/28, p. 1.
40. Beal, op. cit., p. 104.
41. *Evening Standard,* 7/31/28, p. 1.
42. Ibid., 7/31/28, p. 1.
43. Ibid., 8/9/28, p. 2.
44. Fall River *Daily Herald,* 8/9/28, p. 1.
45. Ibid., 8/15/28, p. 2.
46. *Evening Standard,* 8/25/28, p. 1.
47. Ibid., 9/10/28, p. 6.

CHAPTER VII

1. *Evening Standard,* 5/23/28, p. 1; 5/26/28, p. 1.
2. Ibid., 7/14/28, p. 2.
3. Ibid., 8/8/28, p. 2.
4. Ibid., 8/8/28, p. 2.
5. Ibid., 8/9/28, p. 2.
6. Ibid., 9/9/28, p. 2.
7. Ibid., 9/9/28, p. 2.
8. *Daily Worker,* 9/14/28, p. 1.
9. *Evening Standard,* 8/6/28, p. 1.
10. Ibid., 8/11/28, p. 1.
11. Ibid., 8/11/28, p. 2.
12. Ibid., 9/19/28, p. 9.
13. Ibid., 8/25/28, p. 1.
14. Ibid., 9/26/28, p. 6.
15. *Times,* 9/27/28, p. 1.
16. *Morning Mercury,* 9/26/28, p. 4.
17. *Times,* 9/28/28, p. 1.

18. Ibid., 9/27/28, p. 1.
19. Ibid., 10/1/28, p. 1.
20. Ibid., 9/28/28, p. 2.
21. *Morning Mercury,* 10/1/28, p. 6.
22. *Evening Standard,* 10/3/28, p. 2.
23. Ibid., 10/1/28, p.1; 10/3/28, p. 2.
24. *Times,* 10/2/28, p. 2.
25. Ibid., 10/2/28, p. 6.
26. Ibid., 10/2/28, p. 1.
27. *Evening Standard,* 10/3/28, p. 2.
28. *Times,* 10/3/28, p. 6.
29. Ibid., 10/3/28, p. 1.
30. Ibid., 10/3/28, p. 6.
31. Ibid., 10/5/28, p. 19.
32. Lahne, op. cit., p. 214; Papandreu interview.
33. *Evening Standard,* 10/6/28, p. 1.
34. Ibid., 10/8/28, p. 2.
35. Ibid., 10/8/28, p. 1.
36. Ibid., 10/9/28, p. 1.

CHAPTER VIII

1. *Evening Standard,* 10/9/28, p. 1.
2. Lahne, op. cit., p. 253.
3. *Evening Standard,* 10/9/28, p. 1.
4. Papandreu Interview.
5. *Times,* 10/10/28, p. 6.
6. *Evening Standard,* 10/9/28, p. 6.
7. *Evening Standard,* 3/6/29, p. 1.
8. Ibid., 10/23/31, p. 1.
9. Papandreu interview.
10. Beal, op. cit., pp. 109-352; Bernstein, *The Lean Years,* pp. 20-28.
11. Belfridge, *The American Inquisition.*
12. *Standard-Times,* 3/16/50, p. 1.
13. Conversation with Mary Figueiredo, 5/25/83.
14. Fauteux interview.
15. *Evening Standard,* 11/15/28, p. 19.
16. *Evening Standard,* 6/20/29, p. 9; Wolfbein, op. cit., pp. 118,
17. Ibid., 8/12/34, p. 1, 14.
18. Ibid., 8/13/28, p. 14; 8/16/28, p. 1; 8/19/28, p. 3.
19. Ibid., 9/11/28, p. 1; Lahne, op. cit., p. 224-231.
20. *Evening Standard,* 9/23/28, p. 2; 9/11/28, p. 1.
21. Ibid., 9/22/28, p. 1.
22. Ibid., 9/22/28, p. 2.
23. Ibid., 4/24/28, p. 1; Lahne, op. cit., p. 230.
24. Lahne, op. cit., p. 266.
25. Wolfbein, op. cit., p. 136.
26. Ibid., p. 141.
27. Ibid.,p. 156.
28. *Morning Mercury,* 5/6/38, p. 1, 2.
29. *Standard-Times,* 1/26/41, sec 4.
30. *Standard-Times,* 3/31/43, p. 2.

INDEX